The Day I Died but Now Live!

The Day I Died but Now Live!

Serenia Farrell

AuthorHouse™
1663 Liberty Drive
Bloomington, IN 47403
www.authorhouse.com
Phone: 1-800-839-8640

© 2012 by Serenia Farrell. All rights reserved.

No part of this book may be reproduced, stored in a retrieval system, or transmitted by any means without the written permission of the author.

Published by AuthorHouse 08/17/2012

ISBN: 978-1-4772-5202-4 (sc)
ISBN: 978-1-4772-5204-8 (hc)
ISBN: 978-1-4772-5203-1 (e)

Library of Congress Control Number: 2012913259

Any people depicted in stock imagery provided by Thinkstock are models, and such images are being used for illustrative purposes only.
Certain stock imagery © Thinkstock.

This book is printed on acid-free paper.

Because of the dynamic nature of the Internet, any web addresses or links contained in this book may have changed since publication and may no longer be valid. The views expressed in this work are solely those of the author and do not necessarily reflect the views of the publisher, and the publisher hereby disclaims any responsibility for them.

Acknowledgements

Anyone in contact with me knows that I love to tell the stories of my life. In many of my conversations I like to include stories from my life to share with others. This book is a collection of some events from my life. Some might not agree with every detail but everything is honestly told according to my interpretation and what I remember about each event. I was divinely inspired to begin and continue writing this book. It helped me to deal and heal in different areas of my life. I'm a true believer in that God has a purpose and plan for everything. I believe that everything that I have been through in my life was to help mold me into the woman that I am today. I am a woman who can relate to so many issues that children have to deal with growing up and issues that adult women need to address. All of the pain I endured able me to feel the pain of so many people and has given me the desire to want to help. Even if it means sharing my story so others can see that you can move pass difficult things that life offers. If God could do it for me He can do it for you! My hope is that every person who reads my story life is impacted in a powerful and positive way.

I want to thank God for being God! For never leaving me or forsaking me! For being my all and all my everything!! Jesus! I would like to thank my incredible strong husband Wayne for praying for me, teaching and loving me! My very talented son Nashon for all his help and listening to my dreams and not knocking them. My two beautiful daughters Nyla and Milan who drive me to be the best I can be. Thanks to my Pastors Cassius and Mary Farrell for covering us! And the entire family Gizelle, Geremy, and Jordan for all there help. Thanks to all of my family through out America and Trinidad. Shout out to Albert, Kenyata, and Kadir. My precious Pastor Barbara Glanton in which I can write a whole book of gratitude for all that she has done for me and to the entire Glanton family for accepting me into their family especially my Cyrenthia for listening to these stories over and over again! Thanks to all the families that made me apart of there's: The Hampton's Aunt Linda, Lynn, Sa and Gerald. The Thomas family especially my Suzi for always being there. All the Farrell's, my church family, my coworker's special thanks to Glenda Pratt for always encouraging me to complete this book and believing in me! Every person who was included in my stories willingly or not! Every person who ever helped me along the way! And a host of so many others I love you too! Last but not least you for reading my story!! Be Blessed!

Special Dedication

To my family sitting in heavenly places! My momDelores Redmond for doing her best. My Sister Theresa for tagging me along! My Brother Melvin whose birthday calls I missed the most! And my cool Uncle Hamp! My Grandma Louise Klein, My Granddad Eddie Winberly. *Rest in Peace!*

Chapter One

"The Dying Experience"

Jesus answered and said to him most assuredly I say to you, unless one is born again he cannot see the kingdom of God! John 3:3

Have you been searching for something and unsure of what you're searching for? But deep down inside you know there must be an answer! The truth is we all search in different places and in different ways but there is one answer waiting for us. I once was searching. I mean I was looking high and low and didn't even know who or what I was searching for. All I knew was I wanted PEACE, LOVE, AND UNDERSTANDING ABOUT LIFE.

Do you know what I was looking for was there all the time? It was just waiting for me to ask Him for help. His name is JESUS! He knew one day I would get so lost trying to find Him that I would cry out for help. But I didn't know he would be right there to save me. I was so busy looking in all the wrong places. I couldn't hear Him knocking at the door to my heart. He said in REVELATIONS 2:20

"Behold, I stand at the door and knock: if any man hear my voice, and open the door, I will come in to him, and will dine with him and he with me."

I so was thirsty for the truth that I was spending all my time trying to figure things out. Funny thing is we all try to figure things out because we want to know and won't stop until we find it. But what happens is, while we're searching in places we think are right, we learn it's only a deception by our enemy to pull us further away from the truth. My eyes were opened once I found the truth. WOW! Life for me had shifted to a different scenario. I really saw how the enemy tried to keep me from the truth, knowing I would no longer be in bondage to him.

I know I am not by myself when it comes to searching in the wrong places. There were many mistakes I made. My mistakes might help you see the truth and hear that knock at your heart.

In our search for peace, love, happiness and joy we can mistake many temporary fixes such as relationships, sex, parties, drugs, and money as our answer! Well I can tell you none of these things are the answer to living a fulfilling life.

When it appears that we are alone in this world, we typically look for company. Some of us may run to the hottest club just to be around other people or even to meet somebody to take home. We might also go to have fun to get our minds off the loneliness by dancing and singing to get that temporary feeling of joy. But at the end of the night you are exhausted! Disgusted! And sometimes busted! Dizzy from drinking and drugging, disappointed if you didn't meet the right person.

You got nothing out of that just a hangover and some broke pockets because you spent your last dollars getting in, on a new outfit, hair done (which is all sweated out now) and buying drinks all night! You might come home with a phone number, maybe from somebody that is in worst shape than you. That doesn't sound like any fun. We are so desperate to find the answer that we go to extreme measures and actually believe we "like" doing these things. Just like drugs, we may feel good temporarily then eventually go into a slump still looking for answers.

All the good you think drugs do, it only makes everything much worst. You get depended on it and always going for it when you should go to JESUS! You think you're using the drugs but they are really using you. Look at what it does when you need some love, comfort, answers, and peace. What do you get for a response? What does it do for you? Deceive you by giving you that temporary numbness, lying to you making you think just for that moment that it's all right and telling you "Take some more of me it's going to be all right." Then what do we go and do? We spend more money on drugs that we don't have, wondering why we're upset in the first place. So, now that we see that these fixtures that appeared to be the answer are not. What do we do?

Well, let me tell you what I did! I went to the ultimate club called church! Now this was one club where I did not come out exhausted and disgusted. My answer was waiting for me at the door. Jesus was his name. I was kind of shaky at first because I had never seen anything in my life like this. A large room filled with people who were mostly my age having a good old time listening to this beautiful, mighty woman talking. I was curious. Right away I wanted to know what this woman was talking about that was so good that people were continually clapping their hands, stomping their feet and jumping for joy! I thought to myself I finally found the answer I have been looking for. These people have something I need right away.

To my surprise, the woman was talking about Jesus!! Everyone in the church seemed to have a relationship with Him. They knew I didn't know Him because I wouldn't have been able to sit there calm like that. So, they asked me if I wanted to meet him. I was so happy that I started crying tears of Joy! They told me he loves me unconditionally and all I have to do is ask him to forgive me of all my sins. He did! Then I heard the knock and I opened the door and let Him into my heart. I accepted Him as my Lord and Savior and he saved me. Jesus saved me from all that sin that kept me down and from that long journey of searching. Oh! There's more!

I eventually joined in on the party that was going on. This was the best time ever. I started clapping my hands, stomping my feet and jumping for joy. OH! We were just praising and worshiping Him for what he did for all of us especially for his unconditional love. But wait there was something else in store better than any drug I ever had. It's the HOLY GHOST! You talk about good! It was potent. I was so high! The best part about the holyghost is you can get it at any time just call Jesus! Once you try it I promise you're hooked.

What a night! I left out of church so blessed, free, peaceful, and joyful and I even took Jesus home with me. As I finally made it in my bedroom Jesus told me he would never leave or forsake me. This was the beginning of the best relationship I ever had. He reminded me that all things come from our father GOD up in heaven, which sent him, JESUS!

When he told me that he loves us so much that he was crucified and had died for our sins, so that we could have eternal life he said he would take care of me give me unconditional love, he would teach me, keep me happy and satisfied. He didn't want me to worry about anything and to let him handle all my troubles. I was so amazed. All I had to do was obey his commandments and listen to him. I had no problem with being obedient to him because I had been obedient to men before and they didn't offer me any of those things. This was just the beginning of a loving and genuine relationship. All I had to do was trust him, believe in him and be obedient to him. I decided I would do those things unto him just for the love alone, that he has for me and because I can never love him as much as he loves me. I would delight myself in him. The bible said *in Psalms 37:4:"Delight yourself also in the Lord and HE shall give you the desires of your heart."*

June 2000, one day after work, I got off on the wrong exit to come home. I don't how I missed my normal exit. I ended up in front of my girlfriend house from college in Harlem. We used to always get into deep conversations about God and religion in college. When I pulled up to her house she was outside ready to talk. I explained to her that I was not happy.

At that time, I was engaged to this young man I was living with and we had a pretty good relationship. I didn't understand why I wasn't happy because I always thought if I had a good man I would be set and good to go. I was wrong. My girlfriend started telling me in a roundabout way that I had a void in my life and that I needed JESUS.

She invited me to go to her church with her in Newark, New Jersey. I said reluctantly, "Okay I'll go".

I proclaimed to be a Muslim. Yes a Muslim. So for me to agree to attend church it had to be God. The next day, which was a Tuesday, she called me about 6 o'clock. I was too high to go to church! She understood and offered to go maybe next week.

One day during that week I got up early one morning and got on my knees and said to God, "I know you are real I just don't understand all these types of religions," I continued "Please guide me in the right direction I want to be right with you!"

After that prayer I felt so light and at peace. Yes, God had begun working in me. That next Tuesday my girlfriend called again around

5o'clock and said she was down stairs to pick me up for church. It was a miracle because I was not high. I felt like I had no choice but to go now. It was my time. When I got to this building in Newark I experienced what I shared with you earlier.

The pastor asked if anyone wanted to give their heart to JESUS. I was standing still but the devil was saying to me don't go out there, you're playing with God, you don't know what you're doing! I didn't know then that the devil was a liar so I continued to stand.

The pastor stood in the pulpit and said, "There are three people that need to give their heart to God.

She pointed at one man, then another and then I was the third. She looked deep into my eyes and said it's not about religion it's about a relationship! He heard and answered me. I knew this was God speaking to me and answering the prayer I had prayed. He was so real. I walked to the pulpit and gave my heart to Jesus! Instantly, the old ME died right there. I was never the same after that day. It wasn't easy getting to this point. This memoir tells of my story of the journey of getting to this place of letting self-die in order to really live!

Chapter Two

"The Womb"

"Before I formed you in the womb I knew you. Before you were born I sanctified you; I ordained you a prophet to the nations". Jeremiah 1:5

I don't remember anything in the womb but I do know that the devil was nervous and I was being strengthened to fight this fight. After only seven months, I entered into this world on September 27, 1972. Seven is the number for completion. I was ready for the world already because I came out feet first showing the devil he was under my feet. I was also kicking his butt! He tried his best to kill me, steal me from my mother and destroy me by breach childbirth. But everything the devil meant for evil, God turned it around for good. God definitely had his hands on me. He said he knew me before he formed me in that womb and he did. My father was the one who took care of me from the day of conception. There was nothing being done in the natural. Why did everything seem against me and I wasn't even born yet? My mother had not seen a doctor until it was time for me to break out. Yes I literally mean break out. I had to due to the drug doses that were entering into the womb.

God literally placed His loving and protecting hands upon me in the womb. He is the reason I made it through childbirth! While in my mother's womb I had to always fight battles. My mother had a disease called Drug Addiction meanwhile never had any prenatal care. It was that old nervous devil trying his best to let my battles destroy me but it was not good enough! No weapon formed against me shall prosper! When my mother returned home from the hospital everyone was surprised to see me. No one knew she was pregnant. So of course my family labeled me as a mistake. When I came home, my uncle's wife made me a little bed from one of the dressers draws. If a manger was good enough for Jesus then a dresser draw was fine for me. My brother and sister were eleven and twelve years old and there was still no father in sight. But I was no mistake. God doesn't make mistakes He formed me and sanctified me and had a purpose for my life. God definitely had a plan and a purpose.

At two months old we lived in a different apartment with my grandmother. My grandmother spent little time there. She lived at her job on the weekdays with a Jewish family doing domestic work. On the weekends she would bar hop. One of my grandmother's partners was our new landlady. They were pretty good friends so was my mother and the landlady's son. But they were partners in the street life. My mother and a man I considered my uncle were very close and into heroin. There was no romantic interest between them. Their friendship was almost like two best girlfriends even down to the urging and fighting. It got so out of hand that one day my mother busted him in the head with a hammer.

The police showed up soon after to arrest my mother. I'm not sure if thy came this time for what my mother had done recently or another illegal activity. The police was going to call the state agency to come and get my brother, sister and I. The landlady was the one who God touched to keep me for two years until my mother was released from prison. My grandmother came home on the weekends and helped financially with what little she had. Do you see how God kept me? Through it all I could have been in foster care all messed up somewhere. That landlady became my godmother because she was God sent to protect me. It wasn't easy for her but she did a good job and I thank God for her.

Chapter Three

"In the Beginning"

"So banish grief and pain but, remember that youth, with a whole life before it, still faces the threat of meaninglessness"
Ecc. 11:10

I can vaguely remember me at three years old. I remember the apartment we lived in and making mayonnaise sandwiches when I was hungry. There were times it wasn't even enough to make a mayo sandwich. My mother had been recently released from prison trying to make it on her own with her three children and new countryman. We stayed in that apartment for a short time and moved around the corner to a bigger apartment that my cousin accidentally set on fire one day while visiting. That's when we moved to the hotel.

The writing of this book is really taking me way back. I definitely remember living most of my childhood in this welfare hotel located

The Day I Died but Now Live!

downtown Paterson, New Jersey in the shopping area. My grandmother lived in room 408 for the longest. We moved around a couple of times throughout the hotel. It seemed pretty fun living there especially since it was next door to a movie theater.

The cop that worked as security would let my friend and I in every Saturday and we would watch every single movie before we went home. We enjoyed karate movies the most. We would come home kicking and swinging moon chucks like we were Bruce Lee or one of the kung Fu stars. I remember wearing Chinese slippers and carrying moon chucks and ready to go at it! Sometimes he would forget I was a girl. One time he even kicked me in my private part, which was really a reality check that I was not Mrs. Bruce Lee.

His name was E and I'll never forget him because we were all we had. There were not that many children living in the hotel. His mother did her thing and mine did hers. We were very young with lots of energy and we sure put it to use. We would sneak up on the roof of the hotel and drop down water balloons on people. E and I would go to this lady's room we called Crazy because she would yell and talk to herself. She always yelled, "Down, Down, Down, up down the elevator!" She would never close and lock her door. So when we got bored, we would snoop around in her room and mess it up a little. We knew that hotel inside out from the roof to the basement. We had a lot of freedom to just roam around and explore.

E and I went to different schools. I would walk by myself two blocks to city hall to catch the public bus to kindergarten. Every morning a little, sweet, faithful crossing guard would be waiting with her big smile to cross me across the street. I made it on time most of the time but I was hardly picked up on time. School ended at 2:35 and I would be there sometimes to 4 and 5 o'clock waiting for someone to remember to pick me up. The school security officer was always so patient and nice to me. I stayed in that school until third grade. It was one of the better schools in the neighborhood considering it was across from two sets of projects. The teachers I had were very nurturing and I learned a lot of things I wasn't learning at home. That's why my career is so important to me because God allows me to pour into so many young people lives the way my teachers poured into my life. I guess that's one of the reasons why I became a teacher. My first permanent teaching position was at that same school I attended as a kid. My kindergarten teacher whom I loved so much was still there along with a couple of other teachers who remembered me. One time I was on a one-day assignment at another school and bumped into my 2nd grade teacher. She was so proud she started gathering up other teachers to come see me, telling them I was her old student that was special to her because we shared the same first name.

In the early years of my life I really don't remember spending a lot of time with my mother. She was always heavy into the street life. My grandmother and sister were the ones who really took care of me. My grandmother was still was doing domestic work but not living there. I would go with her sometimes and would be so amazed at how big and beautiful those houses were. My perspectives changed just from being with my grandmother.

I would play in a big backyard all by myself. I was able to go into the refrigerator and have so many choices to choose from. I remember sitting down having a snack with my grandmother. We would eat toast with cream cheese. That was a treat because we didn't buy name brand food in our house. My grandmother was an alcoholic but sharp! She had these heavy sprayed wigs she would wear with her suits looking like she was rich. That was her thing. She dressed and drank. She would dress me up in fancy dresses with a shawl to match and take me to the bar with her. I would sit up on those bar stools like I was grown and drink Shirley temples and play Teddy Pendergrass on the bar juke box. My grandmother loved Teddy Pendergrass.

Most of the time, my grandmother was in the bar across the street from the hotel or the bar that was in the hotel. One afternoon I even went with her to the go-go bar while some ladies were dancing naked. I remember this because I was traumatized from seeing so many naked women. I had never seen breast or any of that private stuff before. Sometimes when she was in the bar downstairs I would stay up stairs and play with E. If we were really having fun we would take money we collected to my grandmother to buy more drinks, so she would stay longer. She would get so drunk sometimes that the people at the front desk would have to bring her upstairs and I would have to get her undressed. She would fall off the bed and I tried to put her back into it. It was scary but God gave me the grace to get through it. I miss playing with her wigs and how she would cook short ribs and mashed potatoes on a hot plate.

My sister was a teenager, beautiful and such a giver. Even though she was a teenager she had a bar she hung out at too. She even became a barmaid. I don't think they had strict laws back then like they do now. Her best friend lived across the street from the bar. Her house was the place to be. It was a house full of kids while the grownups went to the bar to party.

We would have our own party playing all types of games, telling stories, dancing and doing what kids do. Sometimes when things got out of hand at the house, we would rush to the bar and ask somebody to get one our relatives. I'll never forget the time I was the one in trouble because somehow I put hot sauce in my cousin's eyes. We're not really related but since I spent so much time at the house; they played a big part in caring for me that they automatically became my family. Even after my sister and her friend began to take separate paths, I could still depend on that family, even years later down the road. My mother went back to prison and I had to stay with them again.

Chapter Four

"The Younger Years"

"From my earliest youth my enemies have persecuted me, but they have never been able to finish me off "Psalm 129:2

After years of living in the hotel we finally moved. We moved closer to the area where I was being raised with my other family. This area was mostly populated with Puerto Ricans. There was a row of garden apartments across from an armory. My next-door neighbor was a big time drug dealer and had a girlfriend that was sixteen years old. He was much older. Since he was in that certain kind of business she couldn't have many visitors. They had a big Doberman pincher to guard the apartment. The dog was use to me because I would keep her company a lot. To me she was a lady but now I know she was just a little girl in bondage. She was very sweet. She bought me a couple of outfits. I don't know if she felt sorry for me or she didn't want me to tell she was feeding me cocaine. I guess she felt I was old enough to understand. I was in the third grade and I believe she dropped out of school.

Today I know she was a very hurt girl because she just got deeper and deeper into drugs and they eventfully killed her. At the time I didn't feel like I was doing anything wrong because everybody around me got high. I remember finding a joint one day and taking it to school and telling my friend to meet me at my house after school so we could smoke it. We took turns watching out for my mother while the other smoked in the bathroom.

When my mother came home after she used the bathroom she came up to me and asked me, "Who came by?" I said "Nobody."

She pulled out what was left of the joint and the wooden match we used from out of the toilet. The toilet was broken so it didn't completely flush. My mother took her home and told her parents what had happened. But she didn't really get in trouble. All her family did was smoke marijuana. Even when I would stay with her by her house she would roll a joint with all of the roaches (marijuana butts) they had saved in jars. She and I were close; we were the two girls in the house where we all stayed. I had learned a lot from her, whatever she learned about life she would share it with me.

She was the first one to explain to me what a menstruation was being very descriptive with it. She was also very popular in our neighborhood because she had a very hip nickname, so all of the adults knew her name and this continued as we grew up. People who didn't even know her knew her name. This explains why she had such an influence on me. I valued her opinion of me because she was the one who was "cool". Since she was always teaching me stuff I assumed she knew all the right answers.

At this time we went to the same school. I always had some type of struggle with school. She had been retained before so she was in the grade below me. I would hear the teachers say how bright she was. This added to my impression of her, not to mention she had everything a kid could want. I mean every type of name brand clothes to every toy that was advertised on TV. She would have a birthday party every year and had grandparents that owned a big pretty house on the better part of town. So even though we were the same age I looked to her for approval in whatever I did.

I started fourth grade at the bigger school and she went on to catholic school. It was now time for me to move on to the next apartment. We moved on the other side of the city. I didn't know too much about this side. It was a little culture shock for me. Where I came from it was highly populated with Hispanic people. So naturally I picked up some things from their culture for instance my hair was the same type as theirs. I would wear my hair out like them. But when I went to the new school on the other side of town there were very few Hispanics. I mean very few. I really stuck out like a sore thumb because not only did I pick up some culture I actually looked like a Hispanic. I couldn't wear my hair out any more. They would want to play in it or pull it. Even the boys would pull my hair. A lot of girls had already had relaxers and you could tell they didn't take care of their hair because it was falling out or fell out. So a girl like me being a student with long hair and what society calls nice hair was really noticeable. It was so noticeable that everyday someone wanted to fight me.

We would line up to go home and girls in other classes that I didn't even know would give signals that were saying "I'm going to get you!" My response would be, "what did I do now?" So every day it was something. The class work was different. They had already learned cursive writing so I had to teach myself how to write cursive to catch up with them. My handwriting today proves I did this! I had to teach myself a couple of things like tying my shoe and do you know while living at this apartment I taught myself how to ride a bike? I was eleven years old just learning how to ride a bike! I also had to go through a lot with the girls on my block. Time went by and things got better. The adults were even out there fighting each other so you could imagine what their children were like. It was different living here it was almost like living in another town.

One thing I liked about this apartment I had my own room. We had it pretty good when we lived here. My mother was still collecting assistance from welfare and she had just finished cosmetology school. So she had an under the table paying job doing hair and still hustling her drugs. She had no shame in her game. My mother would mix her coke and bag it up right in front of me. That's how I knew what she was doing. Back then it was no big deal to me it was just a part of life. But today it's amazing all the things I saw and did at an early age. At this time I was able to get a couple of name brand things. This is when Lee jeans, Pumas and name buckle belts were popular; you also had to have a shirt made with your name ironed on it. I was really excited that I had a few of these items.

By Christmas all I wanted was a sheep skin coat and nothing else. You know by now my girlfriend across town had already had two and I had to have at least one. I really thought between my mother and grandmother I would get one. Christmas eve I saw my mother come in with a big puffy package. I just knew it was my sheep skin coat. I called all my friends and told them that I had one. Well to my surprise it was not a sheepskin coat. It was a coat with a hood and fake fur inside and my grandmother brought me a nice fancy coat like I was going somewhere fancy. I was so mad! That was just like my grandmother she always had to be fancy. I was just too through with them.

As a fourth grader I was really beginning to become more curious and ready to explore more things. Since I had so much freedom I would skip school when I felt like it. One time my mother sent me to school with this plaid print skirt like I went to catholic school. I knew if I went to school they would have a field day cracking jokes on me. So I decided to play hooky with this new girl.

She was a pretty girl that I'm not sure of what she went through I just knew she came from a large family and was already an aunt. I didn't know too many children who were exposed to the things I had been exposed to so meeting her was rare. She was just as hip as I was or probably more. So we played hooky that day walking around a suburb of Paterson. We even walked alongside the Passaic River smoking leaves. One day she stole a bottle of wine that was close to the door of a liquor store and we drank it. But that was it for me with her. A girl who was like a big sister saw us together and warned me not to hang around with her anymore. I knew I would end up in deeper trouble if I continued to hang with her.

Living on this block was fun at times. One of my friend's mother, boyfriends would ride us on his motorcycle up and down this huge hill. We had a lot of fruit trees in the neighborhood and always had fruit to eat. Once my mother had put together a block party and my friends and I went around with a list to see who wanted to participate and what they would donate. My mother was doing alright financially.

She would take my friends and me out for ice cream at different places. We would be happy to see that green car turn into the block because we knew we had an opportunity to go somewhere and do something. Some of my friends stayed over on regular bases. One girl was younger than me and had a big family. My mother really liked her and another friend of mine.

One time we got into a big fight and she bit a big chunk out of my inner thigh I still have the mark. The other two girls I played with were cousins and their grandmother was like the mother of the block. She was the one who had the fruit trees and collard green garden in the back where we were not allowed. My friends' family constantly fed us on the block. At one time her family watched me after school until someone came home for me. I liked that because they were a big family and I loved being around families. I would pretend I was apart too. I still do that even to this day.

I have been in so many families. God is so good because I did end up experience that bouncing from family to family thing but it was by choice and not having to deal with the state agency. Thank you JESUS!

By fifth grade I started making friends at school. This is when I begin to form friendships with boys. I was especially cool with two boys in class. I started talking on the phone. We would talk about stuff that happened at school and new songs that came out. One of the boy's older sisters would spend time with me; she's the girl I said was like a big sister. She would expose me to positive stuff. The other was actually the grandson of the lady who raised my mother and uncle. So he was like a cousin to me. See I was still making those family connections.

There was one boy who was in the sixth grade and all the girls liked him. We hooked up some kind of way. On Easter he came to visit me. My sister had an apartment on the third floor and her electricity was cut off so she never stayed there. I had access to the key so when I wanted I could sneak up there as long as I walked soft no one would know because we lived under her and my grandmother lived in the apartment next to her. So when he came to visit I took him up there and to my surprise he did not have the same idea I had. I had never spent time with a boy that I called myself liking before. I didn't know what to expect.

He was introducing me to something new. He started tongue kissing and feeling on me and I just let him. I thought this was what you're supposed to do. He even went as far as pulling my pants down and tried to put it in but it didn't work. However I did let him put hickeys on my neck. So the next day I tried to hide them with band aids. When my brother and sister asked me why I had them on I told them I was just playing around with them. I believe they knew what was up because I had one little one on the back of my neck I didn't notice. I was waiting for my mother to come back because she was taking me somewhere.

After my mother came home and we were on our way out the door they called me over and pulled my ponytail up and said, "What is this?" I automatically froze. My mother walked over and pulled the Band-Aids off. I was exposed. She asked who did this and I stood quiet. She asked if he had messed with me so I said no.

My brother and sister would always gang up on me to get me in trouble because they felt I had it easy compared to when they were coming up. My brother was the one who really beat me. My mother would only beat me if I got on her nerves but I would always fight my sister back. When she was pregnant she yelled at me for skating in the house; she tried to hit me and I kicked her in the stomach with the roller skates. I hated when my mother wouldn't let me go with her. So I got mad and called myself running away.

I packed my school supplies because I was going to the sixth grade and my teacher was no joke and I had to practice my handwriting. I wrote a note saying I ran away and left it on the refrigerator with the door unlocked. My nosey friend happened to go in my house and found the note and went running to my brother with it. But something happened to me I just changed my mind and rushed home before anyone would notice I was gone. To my surprise my brother already knew and I didn't know he knew. I tried to ease myself back on the block when my brother noticed me.

He said, "Go upstairs!" and started beating me with a hanger. When my mother came home I acted like I was sleep so I wouldn't get beat again. There was a lot of drama living here.

My grandmother had cancer and I literally saw her wither away. She was too sick to work anymore so she had to share a room with me. She would be in so much pain she would moan and groan all the time. All her hair fell out and she weighed 90 pounds. I didn't understand what was happening and was not very compassionate to my grandmother. All I knew is I wanted my room back. Well she eventually passed on and I still didn't understand. I had never been to a funeral.

At my grandmother's funeral I stayed at the casket talking, touching and kissing her. I thought it was some grown up thing happening and she had to go to another country or planet. All I know is I wasn't going to see my grandmother again. So I ran up and down the aisle crying. Soon after the funeral my mother was arrested again. She must have been bailed out. There was a fire in my sister's apartment and we were all burned out.

Chapter Five

"Childhood"

From now on, this month will be the first month of the year for you! Ex.12: 2

We moved back to the other side of town and the pretty part to. I had to get transferred again. Every day I use to fall asleep and my teacher would let me sleep; she would tell the other students to leave me alone. In this school the kids were friendlier. I found more hooky partners but they were all sexually active except me. I would just let them use my house sometimes. The boys in this hooky crowd actually became recording artist later in life. One of these boys and his girl had sex so much just like the grownups I was around. My mind was blown away I was so amazed these preteens were getting busy like this. That's what we use to call it back then getting busy. The other girl was just faking like she was doing something so she could fit in. One time we played hooky at my house and I just went from room to room watching them. I couldn't believe it was real!

This girl and I became close friends. I would always stay by her house so I could go to church with her. Her mother was a sanctified woman. She didn't wear pants and all you heard in her house was gospel music and prayer going on. This was something new to me. We couldn't do certain things in her house like call boys and stuff like that. It was real strict. Literally, all they did was go to church.

I don't know how it all got started but I started going to church all the time too. I started to learn religion and wanted to live like this too. I was so into it I remember hearing her mother beating her for something and asking, "Why can't you be like Serenia". That scared me and I felt sorry for her. I cooled down from coming over so much but continued to go to church. We went to a church in Paterson and the pastor had another church in Harlem, New York.

Eventually her and her mom moved south. So I started going to the New York church with this couple every Sunday and Friday night. They would pick me up faithfully every Sunday and take me to New York. We attended the first service and then we went downstairs to eat then the night service. I would get home eleven or twelve at night. I was really into it I didn't wear pants, I walked around with a big blue bible, I didn't listen to the radio or watched much TV and if you cursed around me I would plead the BLOOD OF JESUS! Every Sunday I would get in the prayer line to get hands laid on me. The anointing on the bishop was so heavy. Even thou I didn't understand a lot of things back then the power of God would hit me and I would fall out! I didn't shout like the other people would or speak in tongues. I was just doing all the right things but not having a personnel relationship with God.

Around the same time my mother went to prison again. This time she did eighteen months. My sister was left to care for her little boy and me. The apartment was too much for her to handle so we moved again. We moved to the block where she use to barmaid. The family house we use to stay at had burned down. They moved around the corner. I started off with staying with my sister but then she started using drugs really bad. We didn't have electricity for a long time and weren't getting along so I moved around the corner with the family that got burned out.

One thing about this family they would never turn me down. Their house was already overcrowded and they still let me stay. It was a one-bed room apartment with about four or five adults and six kids including me. I slept in a twin bed with my cousin and her two daughters. They fed me every day and made sure I went to school. I was so happy because in spite of my circumstances I was in a family setting. We had fun! We would all sit around and watch TV and drink Pepsi. I was still going to church every Sunday in New York. I had befriended the pastor niece and sometimes I would even spend the night with her. Her family lived in the same building as the church.

I remember one Easter the pastor daughter had brought me a nice dress and hat to wear. I was so blessed that some one cared. Another girl that was older than I would take the bus to New York to church sometimes. She was dating the pastor's son and I had a crush on him so I stayed away from her at first. Somehow God had brought us together and we discovered that her father and my mother knew each other. She took me on the other side of Manhattan to meet him.

He was a known drug addict. All of his limbs were blown up from shooting so many needles. I was a little scared but I was glad to be there for her because nobody else could have gone there with her. This was good for me because I was so into being saved and the religious aspect of it; this was an act of love. Every Sunday I would get on the prayer line for Bishop to lay hands on me. I would always feel the power of God touch me. I would go to revival and tarry for the Holy Ghost but would never speak in tongues. I would never catch the Holy Ghost as said back then and dance in church. I couldn't understand why I couldn't receive those gifts. Now I know it's because I wasn't in relationship with Jesus. I wasn't reading and understanding what I was reading. I was just going through the motions being religious. I didn't know the difference back then.

Well my mother came home from jail and moved in with my sister. She had come home to a lesbian relationship. I started going to my sister's house more which happen to be on the avenue where everything was happening. I would try and get my mother and her friends to come to church with me but they would never come. They would sit around and mock the church people. My mother clearly knew who God was because she would always express" Someone up there loves me." She always wore this gold cross and it was very dear to her. I found out later on that my mother had also had a church going experience one time in her life.

My friend who had such an influence on me came back in my life. She was even more street wise. I went around her and her mother with my big blue bible, long skirts and heels; they thought it was funny. It had really disturbed my spirit. Back then I didn't know when I was little people would say I was cute.

My friend mother would say, "I don't know why yall keep telling her she so cute" and continued on "She ain't going to be nothing but a trick like her mother and sister."

Today those same words she tried to curse me with returned to her and her daughter. This was the devils first attack to break me down. Soon after my visit with them I missed a Sunday from church and that was the end of church!

Chapter Six

"1986"

"Again the devil took Him up on a very high mountain and showed Him all the kingdoms of the world and the glory of them." Matt 4:8

It was the summer of 1986 the summer before freshman year. My friend knew guys that were driving 98's and Seville's and would come ride us around. My mother saw this and began to get scared and tried to get strict with me. She called herself putting me on punishment. But I had already been lured into the devils traps of glitter and glam of the streets. My mother was hanging out with another lady hustler who loved the kids and would talk her out of keeping me on punishment. My mother would stay local helping her. Until one day the man she was dealing for gave her some bad stuff that killed her. Shortly after that my mother moved with her ex-boyfriend. Things calmed down for her but the devil had an opportune time once again to try to kill, steal and destroy me. Since I did not know the word or have a relationship with God I could have been lured into the devils temptations of serving him in the world.

As soon as I came from under God's umbrella of protection it was war for real! After missing just that one Sunday and getting a little taste of what was out there in the world I could not press my way back to God's house! But I believe that this is when God was with me the most. Now that my friend was back in my life I was ready for her to take the lead once again. Our time apart she was exposed to even more, she had been hanging out with older girls and experimenting with all types of drugs and dealing with older guys with the hottest cars. Again, my mother didn't like it but it was too late for her to do anything.

That summer I was exposed to so much! I think the devil tried everything he could to kill me once again. I remember an incident my friend got into with this dude from around the way. He smacked her for arguing with his girlfriend. She was so mad she went to tell the well-respected dudes that nobody messed with in the neighborhood. All the girls loved these dudes too. When we got to their hood one of the brothers asked her who I was. Guys were never really asking for me because I was so skinny and didn't have much. I was shocked a man like this that was well known and ruthless asking for me, I dare not ignore him even thou he was much older. He asked for me to come back around that night to see him, of course I did!

"1986"

Well again I had the surprise of my life, not knowing what to expect but didn't want to miss out on such an opportunity. Well when I showed up he took me up stairs in this room in his mother's house. I was just freshly getting into the smoking and drinking thing. So he smoked a couple of joints and drank a 40 oz. of beer with me. I was so high and scared. He began to kiss me and touch me leading to my clothes coming off. I told him no I never done this before he just proceeded and begin to take it anyway. It was so painful all I could do was stay still and take it at this point. He put these two big hickeys on my neck and sent me home with blood filled underwear. My friend made a big deal like I really did something. I guess I pretended it was something other than what really happened. Now I had a chance to be down, accepted and accepted by a man. Even thou I felt violated I was cool and accepted by my friends. I went back by him the next day and it was an instant replay of what had happen the night before. After the second time I thought I knew what I was doing.

It was no longer just my girlfriend and I. We formed a little crew. The oldest one was like the leader she had a little son. She also had dealings with one of the guys in the hood. She did everything to encourage me to see the brother. For the most part it was us five everyday rains, snow, blizzards even tornados we were outside together! We walked around just about the whole Paterson every day. We started at Park Ave and Summer

Street; went through the whole fourth ward down the hill to North Main, C.C.P projects and back. When we knew people were out in their hoods we would just go through and keep it rolling.

A lot of girls didn't like us but most of the girls had a reputation and was respected so we didn't have to do much of showing it. But one time this girl from the projects wanted to fight me. I didn't want to fight her because it was over this sorry behind guy who I didn't even care about. But she was madly in love with him. When she came to fight me I sprayed mace in her face. Then she went and got all these girls from the projects like they were going to jump me. It was only five of us and about twenty of them. Everybody said just fight and get it over with.

I had a cousin that was from the projects and she was with them and my sister came around too—they said they would make sure it was a fair one. Well I sprayed mace in her face again and again by the third time it was time for us to fight. It was crazy with all those girls around me screaming and yelling. Years later I found out we were related. She is from my mother's father's family.

That guy she was fighting over was my down stairs neighbor and all he did was trick with young girls because he had a little car and money and looked a little decent. I would only be bothered with him to get money. Until one day he took me to a hotel and left me there. He sent one of his friends to come get with me but the guy was merciful and just took me back to Paterson. My crew was like a little family we looked out for each other. We've done so much wild stuff together. One of the girls in the crew knew this bus driver that would pay her just to play around with him and sometimes she would bring us for protection.

On New Year's we didn't have money for an outfit so we took the bus on Route 4 to a store. We went in and put on outfits and walked out. We would scurry all over just to buy a new outfit. But eventfully we got sick of that and started with our own hustle! So that New Year's we got so drunk especially me. We were drinking brass monkey, southern comfort, beer, and Bacardi and were smoking. We took the bus to New York City. We was so wild and drunk we got to the Port Authority and fell down a whole flight of stairs and started jumping in other people pictures. Until this crew from Brooklyn chased us back to the same bus we came over to New York on. So we were only there for less than ten minutes and got chased back. When we got back to New Jersey I could barely walk. They had to lock me in my friend's grandmother hallway so I could sleep it off.

Like I said we started on our own hustle. We started off by holding these drug dealers stashes that was until we started to mess up. My friend stashed some coke bottles in the bathroom in a douche bag and it melted. Then one time I was so paranoid I dropped a whole bundle of dope into a hole that lead to a basement we couldn't get into. Then we started helping other people and before you knew it my friend and I were taking out some to smoke and sell for ourselves. We graduated to knowing how to go to New York and buying our own product and selling it.

We had big plans we were going to buy big gold chains and all. But I couldn't take it anymore it was taking too much time and I could run the streets like I wanted to. So we left that alone and continue to get guys for their money. We weren't like real live prostitutes or anything. We would find guys who had money and get what we needed when we could.

I was working in a summer program at one of the high schools because I was too young to have a real job. One morning we were waiting for the bus to pick us up. I was speeding on a sleepless night because I had been up all night! I had just come back from New York with these local guys who had been feeding me cocaine all night and because they had picked up product they had gave me money.

Unbelievably, I was 13 years old "coked" up with all this money in my pocket buying my other teenage friends breakfast at the store. They had no idea what was going on with me except I was smoking a lot of cigarettes and being really nice. I had so many times like this when I thought I was just going to die because my heart would beat uncontrollably. I had even tried this pill called a tab or mescaline. I heard it's really rat poison.

It cost five dollars and it kept you up all night and makes you hallucinate. The first time I took one the noisy neighbor down stairs overheard us saying we were going to take one. He and his friend called themselves making plans to take advantage of us and my friend mother heard them. So she asked us and we denied it of course. So she made me and my friend go in the house. I couldn't sleep and we still didn't have electricity. But we had a little TV that worked on batteries. I watched TV all night talking to it and spitting out my cigarette smoke. Another time it was about five or six of us who took one of the pills. Everybody was bugging except me so I thought I spit it out so I took another one and drank a beer with it so it could work faster. Well everybody disappeared. I was left walking around Paterson in the middle of the night by myself.

I wound up in the store across from my cousins house pretending I was using the phone. I was so scared because when I called my friend she said that the store owner lives in the store and is going to lock me up in there. He was an old tall scary looking man. Walking in the street was normal for me especially when I moved with my mother to her boyfriend house. It was quite a walk from the block to where we lived and after hanging out all day and night. I had to walk home by myself sometimes. I would walk fast and at least I stayed on a main street, which was always dark because it was late. It would be scary because sometimes men that were drunk would whistle and say fresh things as I passed by.

That summer was a crazy summer because a lot of things happened. It was the beginning of a war for me. In the summer 1986 the devil really tried to kill me again by planting all these destructive seeds of behaviors, drugs, alcohol and sex upon me. I was young and on an exploration doing whatever the devil had me doing. This was my first step into street life and at times I really went beyond the extremes.

Chapter Seven

"High School Years"

"Do not fear, for you will not be ashamed; for you will forget the shame of your youth . . . . (Isaiah 54:4 NKJ)

September came and I was starting dear old Eastside High with Principal Joe Clark. When I realized I had the freedom to go in that building without anyone questioning me I took full advantage. Every day I would go to homeroom and back out the door to hang out. I had no interest what so ever with people in school. I failed all my classes that first marking period.

That was a wakeup call for me so I tried to do better. Living down the street from the high school every summer we would watch the marching band practice. That was my big dream! One day I dreamt to be a part of the famous Eastside High Marching 100 band. At the end of my freshman year it was time to try out but you had to have at least a C+ average.

I had to shape up quick in order to try out. So I did what I had to do and was able to try out. I made it as a color guard. My dream was coming alive! Now I had to maintain that C average. I was more involved in school and was able to make friends with students who actually enjoyed it and lived somewhat of a decent life.

Some of the girls in the marching band lived in a house with their parents. They had their own rooms and phone lines and went shopping on Saturdays with their mom. Witnessing these girls lives made me realize how bad mines were, because up until now I always felt my life was normal. God really used this whole marching band experience to expose me to greater things in life. The whole experience was a blessing that it had a positive impact on my education. I also began to keep better company other than the people on the street.

The advisor on the marching band was the first person I began to open up to. I saw life in a different way. My mind was being bombarded by so much stuff. I had already moved out of my mother's apartment and was paying my friend grandmother fifty dollars a week to sleep on her couch. I had an older boy friend that took care of me but I didn't really care about him so much but I needed to survive.

One day I saw my uncle's wife and I told her what I was doing and she said "I knew I should have kept you."

She offered me to stay with her in the projects. I didn't have to pay her and I could eat whatever was available meanwhile letting me know she didn't have money to buy me materialistic things. Through this whole transition I would tell my advisor how I was feeling. I started getting thoughts of suicide. Life seemed too hard. The advisor was dating the school psychologist and she would get him to talk to me. By this time I was really getting into this school girl thing and really fell for this guy who was new and a basketball star. He also happened to live in the projects right in the next building from me. We went out a few times and I thought he was the cutest thing ever.

He was like a dream boyfriend: handsome, popular, wasn't into selling or using drugs just basketball. It was going good for a while until one day I was absent from school and this girl who was out there but pretty asked him was he going to take me to the prom because they were seniors and I was a junior. My friends came home and told me that she was all in his face and asking him questions about me and she was bragging that he said he wasn't taking me to the prom. So the next day I couldn't wait to get to school to give her the beating of her life. When I arrived at school I searched for her all morning and she knew it by third period.

We met in the cafeteria and I went up to her like a madman asking no questions. We both were suspended for 20 days. After this he would not accept any of my phone calls and then began to date her. I was so embarrassed and felt so stupid. I would look out the window and see them going in and out his building and walking around school all hugged up. So now the love of my life that I never even slept with despised me.

I was just having a hard time with boys because I was trying to deal with more decent guys and not really wanting to deal with drug dealers. Even thou most of my friends even the decent school girls had drug dealer boyfriends that kept them in fresh new clothes and the latest jewelry. I was just trying to make it. The only clothes I had were the ones my cousin gave me or what we would go steal out the mall. I guess I obsessed over him for a while.

Their relationship didn't last so long but it was a slap in my face. After they broke up I felt there was hope. I would go to every basketball game and scream louder than the cheerleaders. When I was home I would look out the windows and see him outside because he wasn't outside much like everyone else. I would hurry and get dressed just to walk pass him and he would pay me no mind.

When marching band season was over I grew distracted. During football season I was focused and doing ok. I kept talking to the advisor and her fiancé. I had to keep talking because I was feeling really low. I started talking to this older guy that hung out with the younger guys he even was friends with my heart breaker.

It was a very secretive thing because I was about 15 or 16 years old and he about 27 with a good job, a nice car and he knew what to say to me to make me feel good. I was so naive and didn't know that all he wanted was to sleep with me. Until one day he put hickeys on my neck that I had to sleep with a turtleneck on in the warm weather. My aunt became suspicious and asked me about it or maybe someone told her. She told me, "Serenia you know all that grown man want from you is one thing."

It made sense but I continued to stay in touch with him for years he even would visit me in college. I always knew he had a girlfriend but I never knew why he cheated on her. I got wiser as I became older and learned a lot from him it's just a shame the lies we were living, sneaking around and all. His girlfriend's brother liked me too. But I didn't care for him at all he was one of those guys I just got money from and we stayed in contact for a while too. He was just as old as him. They were like my dirty little secrets. During the seasons of marching band time one of the girls who was on the marching band with me—her brother liked me, and he actually took me to the prom with him. We had a fun relationship because he was funny but I don't think we took each other so serious. I went to two proms that year my class had a junior prom and we were hanging out with this Dominican girl who had a big time hustler boyfriend in East Orange. So he rented us this big limo and gave us lots of drugs. Boy, we thought we were living it up and grown.

We stayed at the prom about an hour and were back in the limo on our way to the club in New York City. It was the last day for this famous club to be open before it closed down. While all this drama was going on in my life I was falling deeper and deeper into depression. I wanted to die I couldn't take it anymore. I would look out those project windows and contemplate jumping.

"High School Years"

One time I was just too through and went in the bathroom. I started cutting my wrist after two or three tries with no skin broken I said this hurts I have to find another way. I guess the razor was dull! (Thank You Jesus). Another time I wanted to take pills but I went to the medicine cabinet and it was only vitamins there. I was always crying and sad.

There was another day my aunt wrote a note to me about washing the dishes. I always had a hard time with this because my mother never made me do anything so I really didn't know how to wash dishes so good. So every time I washed dishes my aunt always had something to say because it wasn't good enough. Along with the fact that every dish in the house would get used then it would be time to wash the dishes it was over whelming for me. I guess she took it as I really didn't care or wasn't trying hard enough but I only was doing what I could do.

I don't remember anything in detail but I took the note as being very mean because I was going through a lot at the time. I went crying to my sisters friend that I called my cousin and she tried to calm me down and then I called my advisor and she was so upset over the letter that she asked if I wanted to come stay with them. So I packed my stuff and left the projects. I was now moving to Hackensack in Bergen County, New Jersey. Even though they weren't married yet he stayed every night with us. I slept on the couch and her daughter lived there too. This was so new for me living with these educated people. They started teaching me responsibility.

First off, I had to get a job and do what I had to do in school. I had no time for cutting or skipping because he still worked at the school and she had just started a new job in Hackensack. I remember that summer I had summer school. I would take the bus to Paterson to JFK high school stay a few hours and it would be time for me to take a bus back home. By the time I reached home it would be time for me to take a shower and get dressed and go to work at Macy's in Willowbrook Mall. After work sometimes I had to take two buses home because of the time. Depending on the bus schedules they had to pick me up from Route 4. I spent a lot of time in between buses. I learned how to properly spend my money. They weren't giving any handouts away and were trying to teach me some responsibility. I would cry when they would sit me down to try to have a discussion with me because I wasn't use to people talking to me. I took it as I was in trouble. They asked was I staying with them or not when it was time to move to a bigger apartment. I didn't know what to say I just cried.

That summer was over so I put my misery out with buses because I rode to school with him every morning since I had a new job at Hackensack Medical Center. This was my favorite job ever. I was making good money too! We became closer as we rode together every morning. I would talk to him every day about my life, family and upbringing. He was the first person I was able to be honest with about my mother being on drugs.

Never had I been able to tell anyone that. So every day I let out a little. In my English class I had to do a research paper. They told me to pack a lunch and dropped me off at the William Paterson College Library and said call when you're finished. Well I never did a paper before until now. I wrote a real good paper on the drug wars in Colombia. I was so proud of this. They even taught me how to order food in a restaurant. I would cry there too because I would always worry about the price and didn't know what to order. So I was being exposed to a lot and learning too. We had some ups and downs.

I wasn't the easiest person to deal with since I had all these emotional scars. I know it had to be hard for them to deal with me being a messed up teenage girl. Still, I thanked God for them because they encouraged me to take the SAT's and go to college. As long as the home was happy they were able to deal with me. They both had daughters her daughter lived with us and his daughter had certain times of visitations with us.

His daughter was a beautiful girl but was a little chubby and she would say little things to his daughter when he wasn't around. Since I was closer to him and we did a lot of talking. I confided in him and told him what was going on. Well one night they got into a fight. I slept through the whole thing she took her daughter and went to her mother-house. When I woke up in the morning he told me what had happen. I couldn't understand why she left me when she was the one who had custody of me.

Not only that she never called to explain or anything she just stopped speaking to me like I had did something to her. So I stayed with him a little while longer. They were trying to work it out but she wanted me out the house. I could not believe she had all this against me and she was the one who brought me here. At first he stuck up for me but eventually made up an excuse for me to leave. So she could come back. Which was ok they wanted to do that but I just wished they both been honest with me.

That situation did a lot of damage to me with being able to trust. I had nowhere to go again. I called everybody I knew but my cousin from the projects came and got me. My aunt was mad. She felt I was having a tantrum again. But my cousin didn't care and brought me home to the projects again. By now I was in my senior year.

I had been accepted to Ramapo Collage. I went to the prom and guess with whom? The love of my life the basketball star! I was so happy that he was going with me I didn't know what to do with myself. Although he didn't take me to his all I cared about was he going with me to mine! My childhood friend went to the prom that year with her boyfriend so they picked us up at her grandmother house. It was a rainy night but I was happy. Afterwards we went to the hotel. This was the big night I was finally going to sleep with him. WOW, I was so disappointed that it was over before it started.

Graduation was also memorable It was a really bad rainstorm on the day of graduation. So they cancelled until the next day it rained again but slowed down. The stadium was still wet. So we were about to use the other high school that was closer to the stadium. I hated this school because it was our rival. When we arrived I cried so hard and was jumping up and down that our principal at the time Mr. Lighty stopped it and said we can go to our own school. I had a lot of school spirit and loved my school. Mr. Clark embedded this in us over the loud speaker he would tell us that we should stand up for our school. We would protest and walk out when the heat didn't work and all sorts of things. If you remember to tell him he would give you a fruit basket for your birthday. The year I got one I was so happy I remember walking home with it.

I was so proud that I almost fell down walking. But no matter what I was not going to let that basket fall. I landed on my knee and it was such a hard fall I ripped a hole in my jeans. He would take the cheerleaders to dinner in a limo. So I would complain that the marching band worked harder and the students enjoyed us more.

Eventually after the 3rd time of canceling on us he let our band director take us out to Red Lobster. I'll never forget Mr. Clark. The teachers didn't care for him much but the students loved him. I was so hurt my junior year he had open-heart surgery and didn't come back. I wanted him to be the one to give me my diploma on stage. It was special anyway one of the teachers wrote us our own special graduation song for the class of 1990. It was awesome especially since I was the first to graduate in my family!

Chapter Eight

"Collage Years"

To console those who mourn, in Zion. To give them Beauty for ashes, the oil of joy for mourning, the garment of praise for the spirit of heaviness. That they may be called trees of righteousness, the planting of the Lord, that He may be glorified.
(Isaiah 61:3 NKJ)

EOF Program

Ramapo's Equal Opportunity Fund Program (EOF) was finally here. I had heard it was a time to learn responsibility. I had no idea what to expect, what kind of people I would meet? What we were going to be doing? Would I know anybody? Well I did know one girl from my high school that was starting the EOF Program too. We had mutual friends but we didn't know each other well. It was good enough for me that we were from the same area. She was so surprised that I was so excited to actually know someone at college. I guess she thought I was crazy or something because we only had history class together.

I was acting like we was best friends. I guess I knew we would become best friends! Besides everyone was clicked together by towns they were from basically. My suite was at the end of the hall and my residence assistance was so cool. I didn't know too much about sorority and fraternities yet but she was in one.

My roommate was a dyke from Passaic and I was flipping out just knowing that. The next day I went immediately to complain to the Resident Assistant. She said I was being prejudice and what made me think she wanted me they have preferences too. She suggested that I just talk to her, lay down the rules and I'll be fine. I was never exposed to girls my age that was openly gay because they kept it a secret.

Well I thought about what she said and it made sense so I agreed. So I sat my roommate down and told her.

I said, "I'm not like you so don't try any funny business and don't look at me or I will knock your head off."

Her response was "No I know you're not like that and I wouldn't do that!" But with her sense of humor she couldn't resist saying, "but if you were because you are cute."

I didn't think it was so funny because I had to wear long pants and sleeves to bed every night in the middle of the summer. It was hard for

The Day I Died but Now Live!

me since I was so free and wouldn't think twice about sleeping nude but not that summer! I even got dressed in the bathroom! Well, we made it through the summer and we actually became pretty cool. Besides she was from Passaic which was close to Paterson.

Every day I had breakfast, lunch, and dinner in the cafeteria and each meal offered so much food it was like heaven. I never had this option either. So of course I went crazy and ate everything and gained weight like crazy. This was the beginning of my weight issues. We took classes and had meetings all day most people went home on the weekends. We made friends with people from everywhere.

Whether it was the cool girls from Newark, the regular girls from Newark, the few crews from Newark, the prissy girls from Bergen County, the South Jersey girls and bits and pieces of girls and guys from other places. I can't leave out the Elizabeth guys and of course it was us girls from Paterson who was known as the cute girls with nasty mouths!! The incoming freshman seemed normal. But the counselors who were juniors and seniors seemed so corny to us. We would crack on them without them knowing.

Actually I didn't care for most of the counselors. My resident assistant kicked it with me about college life. Actually the girls were pretty okay but two of the guys who later became my brothers are the ones who really got on my nerves. The one who wore his pants rolled up with polo shirts swore he was suave; we cracked on him endlessly because he was so country always talking that black power stuff which we didn't know that much about. He was always trying to lecture me and I wasn't trying to hear it at first but we became such good friends even to this day we are really close. I was even in his first wedding. The other guy was his frat brother that almost got me kicked out of the EOF Program. It was the weekend and we wanted to get our chill on so I thought he was cool and asked him to go to the liquor store for us and he told the director about it. They were going to kick me out, but I was able to get out of it. I told them I didn't want liquor but snacks and that I was use to saying liquor store because the projects I'm from all we had was a liquor store that was the store. The program was over and I learned and met a lot of people and felt I was ready for college. I went back to Paterson for a few weeks before the semester started.

Freshman Year

I thought I was ready! But what a shock did I have. The summer program exposed me to different types of black students from all over with different lifestyles. But I had no idea I had a lot more to see and learn. This college is known as a multicultural college. So it had all kinds of students from all over the world. It was all kinds of students including those with disabilities such as blind students with Seeing Eye dogs, disabled students who talked through computers and even an adult program for older people. WOW! I was being exposure! That was just the visual stuff. It was

The Day I Died but Now Live!

really a whole variety of stuff for me to deal with compared to living in the projects in Paterson.

Some professors had more of an influence over me than others. Every freshman had to take this class called freshman seminar, it walked you through collage step by step from choosing classes to campus life. One lesson I learned that I still practice is never study while lying in bed. Reading already makes you sleepy and your bed makes you even more comfortable. It was a valuable lesson. This professor was a down to earth older brother. He really had an impact on my first semester.

I remember when he had become ill I was really upset and scared for him. It was always so good to see successful intelligent black men. It inspired me to know that if they can do it I could too! The other professor was very serious about education not giving you a break because you were black. The first class I had with him right away he asked us to write an essay. I believe it was about what we know about black history or something like that. I felt so inadequate in this area never mind writing skills. I balled up the paper and walked out! He sent this guy out after me and told him you get that sister back in here. Don't know what he said but it sure got me back in there. We also became very good friends and later I was in his wedding too because he married my best friend.

All this new and positive information was mind blowing! I had to have some outlet. We had fun listening to music and dancing in our dorm room. It was my best friend and I along with this really nice beautiful girl from Brooklyn originally from Trinidad and Tobago. She would show us how to dance to calypso music. The Englewood girls were cool with us and we even had a black girl from Mahwah who was really from Harlem and a few others. When it was a party we were there! I had to get use to the club music; in Paterson we weren't into that too much. WE LOVED HIP-HOP!

My first year was memorable but the first summer had even more in store! That first summer break came and I didn't have anywhere to go. One of the girls from Englewood offered me to stay with her. She said her mother let her other friend stay with her before and she would let me stay. So I went home with her. My plans were to get a summer job and stay busy. But a few weeks after being there I received that dreaded phone call. My cousin had called and told me to come to Paterson now! My friend was on her way to choir rehearsal and I didn't have a ride so my cousin asked to talk to her. When she got off the phone she said let's go and was acting shaky so I knew somebody had died! I just started crying and asked her who was? I just knew it was my sister because of her life style.

When we pulled up to the projects my cousin jumped up and went into the house.

I followed her and when I got to her room I asked who died?

She said, "Your MOM!"

I just fell back on her bed hearing over and over "your mom your mom." I did not expect that one. My grandfather called and said she had

The Day I Died but Now Live!

a heart attack. They found her at the end of her bed trying to make it back from the bathroom. Bragg funeral home had come and got her body. I was eighteen and knew nothing about burying anybody! I went to the funeral home to make the arrangements it took about one week to get all the money. My step father went with me to New York to get some of her things. We found out that she had two places she was staying. There was one in the Bronx and one in Grand Concourse in Manhattan. She was receiving assistance in two Burroughs. So I had to go to Brooklyn and I didn't know much about Brooklyn then. So my friend from college met me and took me to the office. I needed to go to try and get help for the funeral. The funeral home took out as much as they could to make it cheaper. I asked her best friend to do her hair she said she couldn't do it so we got this crack head to do it for a few dollars and he did a good job. I had to switch tags to get a nice dress and I didn't plan on riding in the limo but they let us go for free the day of the service. The EOF counselor girlfriend and I got close. Her parents had some friends at their church that took up an offering for me. I couldn't depend on my brother or sister. My brother was nowhere to be found and my sister was on a mission. My mother's brother couldn't do anything because in the past he had burned bridges with people telling them he needed money to bury is sister. So when it was time he had no one to turn to. I felt bad taking money from her dad because he was on a fixed social security income. But I had no choice a couple of friends sent flowers.

"Collage Years"

When it was time to go in and view the body I was scared and wanted to wait until the people had come. But my cousin and the Englewood girl were on my side to take me in. She looked really well I just wasn't ready to accept it. It took me about five years to really accept my mother was gone!

After all I had to move from Englewood because it was said someone told that I wasn't officially on the lease. I just couldn't understand how her other girlfriend was able to move in when I moved out! That was real damaging to our relationship. I called my best friend and told her my living situation. She said I could stay. I was grateful her sis-in law had two daughters and worked 11 to 7 shifts we were the stay-at-home babysitter. Every night while she worked I vowed I would never be in this situation again!

It was time to go back to school and I was ready to start fresh! I was trying to stay focused and do this on my own strength. But my sprit was yearning for God and desiring to live a holy life! Also on my strength I begin to search and call myself looking for god. I read up on a couple of religions trying to understand why we had so many. My roommate's boyfriend and all his buddies just converted to Islam. His roommate was a Muslim from Egypt and was able to convert them all. I got a hold of this book that explained Islam and it made so much sense to me. I began to put all the pieces together and believed that Islam was the religion for me. Believing I would be living a holy life because I would be covered up and following a restricted diet and praying five times a day! So I began to meet with another girl who recently converted. She would talk and teach me things and told me learn before I made my conversion because once I converted; I would always be a Muslim. I learned how to pray in Arabic. Soon after I went down to Newark to my friend father's masjid to take my Shahaddah (confession to be a believer of Islam).

Now I was a full fledge Muslim wearing he-jabs, fasting on Ramadan, praying five times day in Arabic and my new name was Nailah Zakia Abur Rahman. My roommate was the only one around us who wouldn't convert. She continued to confess her love for Jesus and express her loyalty to Him. Whenever I got the chance I would try to get her to convert and she would always express herself through Jesus! Well now I didn't want anything to do with people who were not Muslim. I only dealt with guys who were Muslim! My friend who father was the imam had a brother that I began to date. I'm not sure if ordinarily if I would have dated him. Basically because he was Muslim I went along with it. He was a really nice guy and took such good care of me like I had never experienced before. But of course I couldn't handle someone treating me so good. He was a nice looking guy but he was a big guy and I also struggled with that. But I believed I only could do it with a Muslim brother. That it was okay. Not understanding I was still doing unholy things! Even thou I was trying to appear to be living this restricted lifestyle I was still fornicating behind closed doors but only with Muslim men. I was still smoking blunts but with my Muslim brothers. We would break our fast not to eat but because we wanted to smoke! This went on for some time and eventually I began to physically break away. Those layers of clothes began to come off and I stop restricting myself to Muslim men. I wasn't praying five times a day but every Ramadan I would try to get back on track. I continued to confess to be Muslim until the day I gave my heart to JESUS! This is when I truly began to live a holy life style! This is a story I will save for last!

College life began to take its course in other directions. I was getting more involved in organizations on campus like African Unity and helping a guy who was pledging a fraternity. There are some things that I am not supposed to talk about, so I won't mention which fraternity. This experience exposed me to what really happens behind the scenes. A couple of girls were chosen to help the guy along in his process to become a full fledge respected member of this fraternity. We would do whatever we had to do for him like daily chores, helping with class assignments, and entertaining visiting big brothers when visitors came on campus it was always a big thing. We would prepare food and drinks. It was fun meeting new big brothers from other schools and some were graduates already. All the girls that were helping got a chance to sharpen their game skills! We would have interesting conversations to keep the big brothers attention on us and not the pledging guys. Once he finished his process all the girls who wanted to officially become affiliated with the fraternity had a little process to complete also. Nothing compared to what the guy went through but not an easy one.

While involved with helping I always knew that one day I wanted to join a certain sorority. I didn't know how or when because this organization was not on campus. One of the big brothers knew I wanted to join. His girlfriend was also interested in joining. She knew some other girls that were interested. They were already looking into how they could get this organization on campus. Eventually some other interested girls surfaced and we formed an interest group and began to do things we would do in the sorority. We had organized meetings and did community service. We contacted the sorority headquarters and they told us the requirements. So we started working on what we could. One requirement was to have a local graduate chapter sponsor us. So we wrote these impressive letters to get one to help us. We had a long list of things to complete along with long periods of waiting until finally we were accepted. It was a lot because not only did we join the sorority but we founded a new chapter in the sorority. While doing this we had to concern ourselves with making a decision that could jeopardize everything. We wanted to not just join but have respect in the sorority and with other Greek letter organizations. We had to seek help to accomplish this. It was not easy to convince them to help us because they too could jeopardize everything. Well eventually all the pieces came together! We had everything covered on both sides and were able to be discrete about everything until it was time for us to announce our great accomplishment of becoming members of this sorority and starting this new chapter on campus. My roommate was also going after her goal in joining another sorority the same semester. So this was an exciting time for our campus. Two major sororities were present on campus now.

After all this hard work we still had hard work in maintaining our commitment to the sorority. Now we were able to engage in the fun activities like parties, step shows, and road trips. This was a powerful experience for me and for the most part remains in good standing with the other ladies. We will always share a bond because of everything we have endured together. However I no longer believe in being a part of a sorority due to scriptural reasons. Also I'm about unity and don't think it's good for women to separate themselves from other women especially black women! I know where there is unity God is there! I want to be where God is!

One of those mornings when I was pursuing finding out about Islam I was going with some girls down to Paterson to a service to get information about this sect in Islam. We never made it down. The two girls and I were involved in a car accident. It had just started raining and those winding roads were a little slippery. The driver lost control and drove into a big rock and flipped the car over. I immediately jumped out of the car and realized my back had this intense burning pain in my lower back. Once they checked the car making sure it wasn't going to blow up or anything they made me lay down. When the ambulance arrived they took all precautions and had me completely wrapped up. They said I could be paralyzed! Once we reached the hospital people from the college started to come see me! I can laugh now but nothing about this was funny. But everybody walked in my room as though there were viewing my body at a wake. They all came in with these deeply concerned faces walking slowly across the room not really knowing what to say. It looked worse than what it was. I looked really scary because of all the stuff they had me wrapped up in. After all the test, and x-rays the outcome was I was not paralyzed but my back was broken! I had three cracks in my spine that need to heal. Thank God it didn't require any surgery. I did have months of therapy and wore a back brace for eight months. I was advised to take the semester off to recover I knew campus was my home and I had nowhere to go to recover and I didn't want to prolong my stay there. So I stayed enrolled with a lot of restrictions. After a week of being in the hospital I stayed in my dorm about a week before returning to class. I was able to work something out with my professors. I would go to class and have to take frequent breaks because I couldn't sit for longer than fifteen minutes. I wasn't able to bend down at all. So my friends had to help me bathe. I could get in the shower but couldn't bend down to wash my legs. I wasn't able to go to parties or dance in my room. This was something we did in the evening to relieve stress. We would meet in my suite and blast music and dance particularly pumping dances. It was torture watching my friends unwind and I couldn't. When it was time to go to parties it really killed me not being able to go. Once I went anyway and tried to dance looking like a robot. Everybody made me go back to the dorm. After months of therapy I was able to remove the brace continuing life as normal experiencing some pain. WOW! Another testimony of what God could do. If God didn't show up where would I be?

While I was finishing my sorority process I received a fifty-two thousand dollar settlement from the car accident in which I had to pay the lawyer one third of it. The first thing I did was ask my friend's father take me to buy a car. This was my first car and I knew it was a little risky buying a brand new car but I knew I didn't want to be back and forth at the mechanic. So I paid cash for a brand new green Honda Civic. My friend father was a big time business man and negotiated a wonderful deal. See how God was a father through him. He said he would be a father to the fatherless. Well buying a green car before my process was finished didn't look so good on my part. But once I was done I was living on top of the world. A girl that never had anything was living large. I had such freedom in being able to come and go as I please since I was driving. I always wanted to be adventurous now I was able to go places I wanted to go. I went to every big Greek event and shopping every day. I had a closet full of new clothes mostly in my sorority colors. I begin to hang out with my big cousin going shopping and doing different things.

At the time she was seeing a guy who was a male exotic dancer. One day she convinced me to take her to see him and at the same time she wanted me to meet one of his friends. This was in the day time during their rehearsal time so we sat in the car in the parking lot of the club. Her friend came out and talked to her. One friend who was there came out to meet me. What a joke! The next friend who was more like a cousin to him came out too and he had an eye patch because he had one eye! Well I went along talking to him and eventually I got involved with him. Every-night we were following them to the clubs they danced at. We even added some other girls from Paterson and started a little click. We were consistent in this lifestyle for a while. My cousin continued to see this dancer but I had moved on to the next one. This one was more like a real relationship. We were together for at least a year! I had never had a boyfriend that long so this was serious. I got really close to his family and even after it was over I remained close to them. Shortly after a year I took all I could take and it was over. We were still cool and would hang out time to time. One time I went with him to dance in a show in Washington DC. These dancers are like little celebrities and at this show a local dancer that traveled up to Jersey to dance was there. I called my cousin to tell her. While on the phone with her he walked passed and was eyeing me up and down. I was so excited that he was looking at me. We drank and enjoyed ourselves during the show. The local celebrity dancer came around and was asking them who I was and they told him that I was with one of the dancers. I guess

"Collage Years"

he didn't care because after he danced and was working the crowd, he paid me special attention without getting into details. He gave me his number but I never called. Months later I was seeking revenge on my dancer so I went to another spot in Jersey where the celebrity dancer worked. He was there that night and I made myself know to him. We hooked up after the party and then we had a little fling for a while. WOW did I open my self-up to get exposed to sexual things I never experienced before. I was so hooked on him that I would drive down to Washington, DC every other Thursday and pick him up to come dance in Jersey. He would either stay the weekend with me or we would drive back to Washington, DC and I would stay down there. This relationship went on for a while when I realized I was bugging and decided to let it go. My days of partying with strippers finally died down.

My life was starting to catch up with me and my emotions were running wild and out of balance. I was experiencing signs of depression and didn't even know what to do. I begin to cry a lot and had become so unmotivated. It got so bad that some days I couldn't even get out of bed. My last semester I had to direct a live show for one of my classes and I couldn't even get out of bed to go do it. I watched it on TV as someone else directed my show! My professor for this class caught me one day crying because I didn't have food and other necessities. He gave me a few bucks to get some food and sent me to talk to someone in the mental health center. I met with the counselor a few time and then she sent me to an outside clinic in Bergen County. At this clinic I actually saw a doctor who prescribed me medicine. We started off with Prozac and then tried a few others. I was never good at taking medicine so I wasn't consistent with it. I guess this is why it never really worked alongside with all the marijuana I was smoking. I was failing all my classes and just couldn't do it anymore. So I withdrew from all my classes and moved off campus but where could I go but back to the hood! After running wild in the hood I did go back part time at night to finish up and get my degree.

Chapter Nine

"Back To the Hood"

"O you afflicted one, tossed with tempest, and not comforted Behold, I will lay your stones with colorful gems, and lay your foundations with sapphires. (Isaiah 54:11NKJ)

After spending all that time in college I felt I had to come home and prove something. Prove that I wasn't a sell out and that I didn't think I was better because I went to college. I continued this life's journey hopping from one thing to another. I stopped going to strip clubs now; I just wanted to hang out! Since I was with my big cousin a lot who lived in the projects I was always there a lot. One day I met the cutest, big eyed little boy! I had to find out whom he belonged to because I want to steal him. I met his mom and I begin to spend a lot of time with him. I would take him places and keep him for weekends. His mother and I started hanging out together she already had her set of friends from the projects I just added myself in their little crew.

When she got this apartment in some other projects I went to stay with her when I left school. Even thou I left school I continued to work as a substitute teacher. So I had some type of income for a little while but summer was nearby. I was just getting by and trying to figure out what I wanted to do. I was just hanging out every day going back and forth to New York every day and going to parties and clubs every weekend. Around this time we were hanging out with these two guys from another hood.

Every night we were doing something exciting they would spend lots of money on weed and alcohol. After a while it came out that one of the guys liked me. We were having a good time and I was starting to like him too. It was like a set up because he is not somebody I would have got involved with or would be attracted to. He also used to be involved with one of my old friends that had a child by him. I didn't roll like that.

It was a long time ago and I didn't think she would care now. Well we got really involved and he would stay with me by my friend's house sleeping on a pallet on the floor. It was this girl who had an apartment up there and she never really stayed there because she hung out on the other side of town. She had offered to let me rent out her apartment. I agreed to rent it out but somehow it didn't work that way. She stayed there too and I had an unexpected guest.

One of my friends from South Africa had sent a message for me to pick her up at the airport. I didn't know when I was picking her up she was coming to stay with because she needed help. She suspected she was pregnant and was scared. She had made up her mind that if she didn't want to keep it and wanted to go to the abortion clinic as soon as possible. So we went to a clinic and discovered she was seven months pregnant and too late to abort it.

Surprisingly, she continued to stay with me at this girl's house. She had nothing and nowhere to go! How could she have a baby? So she decided to have the baby and leave it at the hospital! I was feeling so distraught because I really loved kids. If I had my own place I would have kept the baby. So all we could do at this time was wait. While we were waiting it gave us time to think. It was getting pretty wild around here because I wasn't getting along with the girl who apartment we were in and it was a lot of tension in the air. Not good for a pregnant person who had nowhere to go.

She started looking into adoption and found a home she could stay at until she delivered. I was happy she had somewhere safe to go but I still didn't want her to give up her baby. She didn't want her family in South Africa to know because they would disown her. It was close to the time and I really wanted to do something so she could keep the baby. I reached out to another girl who went to college with us that was from South Africa

The Day I Died but Now Live!

too. My friend didn't want her to know anything because she was afraid that she would judge her too.

    I couldn't worry about that I had to help that little baby. I called her and told her and she was on board to do whatever she had to save that baby. She was even willing to send the baby back home to her parents saying it was hers. So she was able to convince my friend not to give her baby up and found her somewhere to stay with the baby in Brooklyn. Before she went to Brooklyn, she called me one day hysterical because she was in labor. So my boyfriend and I went up to the hospital and I went through the whole process with her! It was scary but I was glad she wasn't alone. That situation in my life was taken care of. Now I had to deal with the living situation.

    It was summer and I didn't have any money and was totally depending on my boyfriend. He was a hustler and tight with his money. Given the situation I was in and he was staying there with me I encouraged him to get us our own apartment or room or something! Well one day the girl finally lost her cool and showed up where he hustled and threw all our belongings at him. It was a bit extreme but at least I was out of there. A lady that played bingo with his mom let us rent a room. I wasn't planning on staying there long and my plans were coming to an end.

    One night he got into something with his baby mother and beat her. She told the cops that a gun was involved and gave them my license plate number. So they came there looking for him. It died down for a little while but they were consistent in looking for him. So we had to move on. He was able to get that settled but this was nothing new to our relationship. It was always some drama with his baby mother or obeying the law. It was very stressful. So I had to be careful not to let anyone follow me home and he was careful moving around outside every day. I would spend time with his mom and dad. His whole family loved me. In spite of the circumstances I always felt he had a deep love for me.

One morning it was starting to snow and I decided not to go to work. It was a knock at the door and it was them, detectives looking for him. They continued to knock at the door as he held me tight and told me not to move or say anything. They talked through the door while my landlady was hollering and screaming to open up! Well they proceeded to kick the door down and he went out the window. They chased him and eventually caught him hiding under a car. He really didn't want to go to jail and he even tried to bribe the detectives as they took him down town.

Back in the apartment my neighbor warned me that they would come and lock me up too for not opening the door I quickly got dressed and ran too. They never came back for me and left me alone. I was grateful and ready to turn over a new leaf in my life. I had already been telling him this was too much for me and I wanted this relationship to be over. He wasn't trying to hear it and I had to be careful since he had such a reputation for beating his girlfriend's up! He never hit me and I wasn't trying to provoke it.

I told him that if he did that it would definitely be over for us. Again I was saved by extreme circumstances. This was the only way I was able to get rid of him. Unfortunately it wasn't a good departure. He would call and I would tell him I was moving on and reminding him that I don't do time. Once you're locked up it was over.

He wasn't trying to hear this until one day someone he knew unexpectedly answered my phone while I wasn't there. Oh this really blew his top because this was a guy from another hood that they didn't really get along anyway. I didn't mean for this to get out. That was a hush-hush thing! Again I found myself with someone I didn't plan on being with. He was even more persistent and was only supposed to be a one-time date that continued on. He knew the situation and was just throwing it in his face that he was in my room and I left him there alone.

No one was supposed to know anyway because he used to be involved with my friend from the projects best friend. They weren't currently together but everybody knew they were a couple. He just kept being persistent and aggravating until I finally agreed to one date that led to multiple dates. I guess I was enjoying the thrill of sneaking around. What was happening to me that I was stooping so low to do these kinds of things. Over time I had enough of him because we didn't even get along. He drank a lot and was out of control! The only thing good that came out of this is he convinced me to be reunited with my old friend who I didn't speak to in years. Her uncle had just died and she needed a ride to go to the mall to get a dress. Unexpectedly she knocked on my door and asked for a ride and we were back as friends instantaneously. I can't say he was objective to this because we all use to be close. In high school she dated one of his close friends and I was with the other. Another reason I shouldn't have been bothered with him. The boyfriend in jail never forgot this and he held on to it for a while. When he finally got out of jail I ran into him at a party and someone over heard him saying he was going to shoot and kill me in the party. So I went over to the guys from the projects for protection. I stayed in the middle of them and was finally able to sneak out!

Now I began to hang out with my old friend again. We even went to the funeral together. I was back at work and needed to get a bigger apartment because my nephew who was in foster care wanted to come home and live me. He was having a hard time and I thought I could help.

I began to meet with is DFYS worker and she eventually allowed him to come stay with me. We started in the studio apartment until one day I came home and caught him in the act with some girl on my floor. I was furious because I wasn't even able to have company like that because he was there. Soon I moved close by into a third floor apartment. It had two bedrooms and a kitchen but no living room. The price was right and on a nice block. It was enough room for us.

My nephew was out the system finally but living with me. He received a check that helped our financial situation. However we did run into some problems with that. Every day the high school was calling me on my job because he was acting up and he wasn't listening to me either. He expected me to give him money but I didn't I used it for the bills.

I didn't do much for him because of the behavior. So one day he decides to take the check and cash it himself. A teacher called me and informed me of this. When he got home I confronted him and we got into a big argument that led to a fight! The police was called and he went back to DFYS.

I rented out the room to one of the guys from the projects for a while. That went okay. Except one night a girl came knocking at the door for him. I let the girl in to find him and another girl in the room together! My bad! I really didn't know anything. The next day he told me what happened. He also got locked up and the room was empty again. My old friend was over all the time anyway and she was living with her grandmother with a lot of restrictions so she rented out the room.

She had met this guy from Brooklyn that was quite mysterious. He had invited us to this big party they were having in Virginia Beach. We left Paterson, New Jersey around nine o'clock that night to make it before it was over. When we were going across the Chesapeake Bridge the gas light came on and we smoked at lease a pack of cigarette crossing that bridge.

When we reached Virginia Beach the party was over. But I was like a kid in a candy store nothing but big ballers with big cars and blinging jewelry.

Of course they were all involved and he wanted me to meet his cousin. Here we go with the cousin thing again. He was cool and had a real job so he wasn't as involved as they were! We spent a New Year's Eve with them. They had brought a whole case of Moet and I got really drunk. They took us to a club and had so much power with everyone that they made people get out their seats so we could sit. I was so scared they would start shooting up in there because them Brooklyn jokers don't play! It was a little scuffle but it turned out ok. The cousin and I were digging each other for a while but again it was time to move on.

We both met new guys that weren't connected. She met a guy who was local and was cool. However I started to date this guy, a friend from college introduced me too from Harlem. We met once before and she went with me and had a lot of negative things to say about him so I was turned off. Then one day I thought about it and said I never really gave him a chance so I called him. We talked about my birthday and he was going to a party that the Wu tang Clan was giving and put us on the list to get in.

Well I always made a big thing of my birthday. So I had a new outfit and hair done in New York. My friend did everything to try and mess it up! I asked her way ahead of time if she was getting something to wear because we were going to this big party. I knew how she was. She said it

The Day I Died but Now Live!

not my birthday I don't need anything new. Well when I was getting my hair done she took the car down town to look for something and came back late with nothing. On the way home she wanted to stop and pick up her layaway and took a very long time in the store.

Once we got home she said she was going to wash and set her hair. We were already running late and had to be there by a certain time. I was so mad I got dress and was going to hang out with my barbershop buddies. But since I was so mad I asked my cousin to pull the car up for me and she drove off with it. This was a minor who had no license.

Well I was done after this! I went upstairs and went to bed and didn't want to talk to either one of them anymore. I didn't even call the guy. I did call him the next day and explained. He was very understanding and invited me over for a birthday dinner. A guy never cooked dinner for me! When I arrived he had dinner all set up nice with a big gift and a giant bag of weed. Well I was too impressed! He had won me over! The beginning of what God would use to lead me to Him!

Chapter Ten

"Mr. Right"

"There is a path before each person that seems right, but it ends in death" Prov.14: 12

This one night of just having an ear listen to me and going out his way to show he cared was the most amazing night to me. He had won me over and I just knew he was Mr. Right. He wasn't involved in any illegal activities but liked to do the things I liked to do. He was into this music industry stuff and was pursuing it with all his heart! He constantly took me out on nice dates to different places. We would travel all up and down the east coast visiting his family. I loved it since I didn't have much family and I loved the South. Just about every holiday we traveled or had some type of plans. He had two daughters who I really enjoyed being around. I loved the idea of being a future stepmother. They loved me too. His family in the South thought I was a great mother image the way I cared for them. There was such a difference between his baby mother and me. She was a real nut case that put him through a lot. Just never understood how he ended up with someone like her. He loved to shop and dress, so we always went shopping together. We always did things with the girls on the weekends he had them. It was like a little family. I admired that his mother and sister were classy, black women supported him very much.

We dated heavily and got really close. I would spend a lot of night in his studio in Harlem. Even though we enjoyed going out and doing thing we equally enjoyed a quite night in smoking and watching movies. We did this for a while and soon found out . . . . I was pregnant!

I was excited! I felt he was a good man and father to have a child by and we were in love and one day would get married. But he started acting a little funny like he didn't want to have another baby. I was scared and didn't want to get stuck raising a child on my own. So I called my girlfriend that lived in Harlem to take me to get an abortion.

I thought it would be over between us. It wasn't over. He was a little upset but I assume he was relieved. We oddly continued on with our relationship. My old friend didn't really approve of him and after my birthday incident we really were going our separate ways but she rented out the room in my apartment. We had tried to look for another apartment but she was being impossible so I left it alone.

Then Mr. Right and I were supposed to get an apartment together. We started looking and we weren't seeing eye-to-eye either. So I went ahead and found an apartment in East Orange. The first one was in my friends building and when I went to put a deposit down they told me to look at the building down the street that was being renovated. It was a beautiful apartment with a sunken in living room and hardwood floors, everything was new. So I moved in and we agreed we would live together.

But he didn't want to give up his studio in Harlem. I explained to him that if we lived together it couldn't be no staying out all night. My rule was if we live together, we should be sleeping together every night because if you stayed out basically you were with someone else.

That winter we experienced a bad snowstorm and I told him he should make his way home before it got too bad. He told me he was on his way to the studio. A little while later he called saying he wasn't going to try to make it to Jersey. I tried to convince him but he wasn't giving in. I will never forget this night. It was one of the worst nights of my life. I was so mad and hurt. That was the hardest I ever cried. But I did something different this time. I wrote a letter to God asking him why? Why my life was so hard and why was I hurting so much? Why couldn't I take the pain anymore? I took some tranquilizers I had hoping I wouldn't wake up. Obviously I woke up and tried to regroup but I had made up in my mind that I wasn't going to let him hurt me anymore and that it was over! I knew he would show up soon after so I prepared myself to keep calm.

When he showed up he had the nerve to have an attitude. I started to explain to him that this wasn't going to work and he had to go. He began to argue with me. I tried to stop him. He continued to argue and before I knew it I had blacked out and smacked or punched him.

I don't really remember what I did. I just knew he was fighting me back and had scratched my face.

When I realized it I began to yell, "You scratched my face I knew you were a fag!"

Now he knew I meant business. He asked me for plastic bags to pack his things. I said, "No."

I knew how much he loved his clothes and I was waiting for him to leave so I could destroy them. As soon as he walked off I began to cut and bleach his clothes. It was taking too long so I went to the coat closet and began to cut and up all his coats. When he returned and saw me with that knife in my hand he was scared and realized I had snapped. He grabbed what he could and got out of dodge. Even after all that I was still hurt that he didn't call or nothing.

Weeks passed and still nothing. Finally Valentine's Day came and he called asking could we to dinner since we weren't dating anyone yet. I went. I ended up staying the night. After that we begin to see each other again but it wasn't the same.

I had got a new car and a new part time job to pay for that car payment. I was doing some temp work up in Livingston. It was with this older guy who did security. He looked like a model and wouldn't have known he was a few years older if he didn't tell me. He was into working out and had a body to die for. He was very intelligent and in school working on a Master's degree. We would talk on breaks and our conversations were about real life things. Again, I was memorized by something different. He would write me poems and framed them.

His conversations attracted me. He came over a few times meanwhile I was so paranoid because believe it or not it was hard for me to be disloyal to the person I was with. I also had to hide ashtrays because he didn't know I smoked. It was a little annoying. Spring break was coming up and I needed to study for my teacher's certification test.

So I booked a villa in the Pocono's and invited Mr. Right and his girls. I struggled back and forth because I didn't want to be bothered with him anymore. It didn't help that I wanted to hook up with this new, intelligent guy. The day we were supposed to leave I called Mr. Right and told him to come over and talk before he went to get the girls. He did and I explained to him I wasn't feeling this anymore and I needed to go away by myself. I knew in the back of my mind I wanted to invite the model up.

I went up and was going crazy up there by myself but it was good for me. After three days I talked to the model man and invited him up. He came up that evening and we lit a fire and it was really romantic; to my surprise he didn't try anything. This made me even more attracted to him. Some time passed by and I asked him why after all this time we have been talking he haven't tried anything and was he interested in me that way? He expressed that he was and even though we would use protection he wanted me to take a HIV test! At first I was furious but then I knew I was good and agreed. After all that we went to engage and he went to use plastic wrap for our four-play. That was it I was done. I jumped up, cursed him out and told him to get out my house. I wasn't getting good vibes from him anymore anyway I felt he was hiding something. Besides I couldn't handle being with someone who didn't smoke.

My neighbor and I started a friendship at work too. I never seen her before but at work we often had discussions and discovered a lot of similarities. She would visit some time and we went walking together at the park. She would try to tell me about Jesus. But I would stop her and tell her I was Muslim. She never gave up leaving leave notes with scriptures on it. Sometimes I was bugging I would answer the door and blow smoke in her face. She even had me listen to Juanita Bynum's, "No More Sheets." I didn't realize I was listening to a preacher!

I was enjoying my single life and hanging out. It was this guy that I would tell my friends I was curious about but wasn't trying to really get involved with. My friend played me out and told him one day. So we started having a little fling. I didn't hear from Mr. Right all that time but one day he called me with sad news. His grandmother had passed. I was hurt because she was like a grandmother to me and I felt for him too because I knew how close they were. The day of the funereal I left my fling in the bed while I went to pay my respects. I was late because I had to take my teacher test that morning.

When I arrived it was time to go down stairs and eat. They had expected me to go sit with him in the front. I wasn't expecting all that. I knew I had to get home because I had left this joker in my house. Mr. Right wanted me to stay with him and go down to South Carolina to bury her. I couldn't go with him but I stayed on the phone with him a lot. This was an opportunity to get things going again.

He began to pursue me again and I went along with it a little and when my birthday came he took me on a trip to New Orleans. It was nice we went on tours and ate fancy dinners with incredible food. While we were down there he pulled out this little blue box and popped the question. I was so surprised I felt he was up to something but I didn't expect that, I accepted. I wanted to be married.

He knew this was the only way he would get my heart back into this relationship. So I was so happy with my Tiffany's platinum diamond on my finger and was ready to make wedding plans. For some reason I couldn't get it together. We started staying with each other every night again. By January 2000, we decided it didn't make sense to keep paying two separate rents. We were together every night and because of the incident before we thought it would be best for me to move in with him. I changed my address, license and everything. I was officially a New Yorker. I was able to make this move because I heard God tell me, "Go you will have a significant change in your life for the better." I thought I was going over here to meet someone else that was rich or famous. I didn't know! But I sure met someone rich and famous. His name is Jesus!

When I was younger I used to come to a church over in New York. I began to have this urge but I ignored it. If I turned to preaching on TV I would hurry and turn it because my sprit would jump inside. One morning I went to get information on how to get a teaching job in New York.

I woke up early and got on my knees and said to God, "I don't understand why we have all these different types of religions but I know that you are real, I want to be right with you. Please direct me in the right path."

That morning I felt so liberated and full of joy. Little did I know my time was running out and God was preparing me for what was ahead? Not too longer after that I was going home and got off on the wrong exit again. When I got off the exit I called my girlfriend that lived at this exit. I was feeling some kind a way and needed to talk. She was on her way out but would come down and talk to me for a minute. I expressed to her how I was feeling and she said words of encouragement and advised me to come and go with her to bible study in Newark. The next day she called but I was too high to go. The following Tuesday she showed up about 5:00 p.m. and it was a miracle that I wasn't high or even for me to agree to go because I confessed to be a Sunni Muslim.

I went that night and it was like Jesus himself came and got me. My life changed right then and there, this is the day I died So that He could live in me. I went home that night and smoked a cigarette not realizing God had delivered me. The next day I went to work and told my co-worker I got saved. One of my friends started crying. I didn't understand and asked her why she was crying? She said you don't know how long my pray group have been praying for you to come to Jesus. I was so touched that someone was praying for me and it worked. I still didn't fully understand what was going on so after work I went to buy a bible. On the way home I usually experienced road rage. This day people were cutting me off and blowing there horn at me and it didn't even faze me. This is when I realized I was changed.

Friday night Mr. Right and I had dinner and I explained to him what I was experiencing. He thought it was a good idea saying now you have Jesus and I have my music stuff. But he didn't really understand. Even though we slept in the same bed I was moving closer and closer to the edge and started getting dressed in the bathroom. I wouldn't even kiss him goodbye He was getting kisses on his forehead.

By Saturday I was up early to attend a church picnic and later to get baptized. When I was baptized I let out such a scream. I didn't know my voice could get so high. That was demons that had to come out and I felt even free. On my way home I realized I was so tired because I wasn't getting much sleep because at night I was worried Mr. Right would try to get into something. This is when I realized God had delivered me not only from weed and cigarettes but sex too.

The Day I Died but Now Live!

I knew in order for me to get some sleep I had to let Mr. Right know we couldn't have any more sex until wedding day. My spirit was new and clean inside and I didn't want to jeopardize that. This week I had happen to watch this tape that the preacher was teaching on how when you have sex you exchanging sprits. I did not want any of those old sprits returning in me! I have been delivered and wanted to keep it that way.

When I arrived at the studio it was some tension because he didn't like the fact I have been spending so much time over at the church already. So he had an attitude.

I was going to just go to bed and not say anything but I heard God so strongly say, "Get up and tell him know!"

He was so mad he went on and on just talking for about twenty minutes.

"Enough I'm going to stay by my girlfriend house until you calm down", I said.

He said, "No if you are going to leave take everything and go!"

I called my girlfriend and she took a cab over to help. Mr. Right was never to be seen or heard from again. I didn't know anything about believing God but now I did. I made it to my girlfriend house and in the pouring, heavy rain made it to my first church service. The devil did his best to try and stop me from getting there. But his best wasn't good enough and I made it all by myself because now He lives in me and I'm able to do anything through Him because he is my strength.

Part Two
Life After Death

Chapter Eleven

"The First Steps"

"Being Born Again, not of corruptible seed, but of incorruptible, by the word of god, which lived and abideth forever."
(1 Peter 1:23kjv)

The next day after giving my heart to God I went to work feeling so free. I was so happy and excited I was telling everyone. One of my friends began to cry. I asked her why was she crying and she said you don't understand. My prayer group has been praying for you for the longest and our prayer was to take all the negative ways the devil was using you into God Glory. Serenia would be on fire and enthusiastic about the Lord and His kingdom. My other girlfriend that I use to go take cigarette breaks with outside had just given her heart to God a few months ago. She still believed God for deliverance while we would go out to smoke. She would just marvel about her experience with God and how he was changing her. Her whole attitude had changed right before my eyes. She had become so humble and used to be more rowdy than me!

I didn't even realize how God was using her to sow seeds into my spirit about his goodness. I was so hungry to know more about God I had to go and get me a bible from Barnes and Noble. I was working in Paterson and living in Harlem. That commute every day was wearing me down and I had road rage so bad that it would feel like a ball was going to bust in my head. One particular day during this ride home was where I really discovered that God had changed me! People were cutting me off breaking in front of me. I didn't even feel the need to yell, scream, and not even point a finger. What I felt was peace overflowing and just let it go! It felt so good.

When I got home that night I was so excited to share with my man everything I was experiencing. I believed God would do the same for him. He was cool with it that night. Thursday I went to a women support group held at the Pastor's house. Wow! I was so amazed at all the stuff God was helping these women get through. I thought my life was bad but some of them had deeper issues.

We watched a tape on sanctified sexuality! The preacher was teaching on how sex is for marriage and that it is a holy thing. He explained how men release and deposit a part of themselves into the woman during sex. The woman who is the receiver housed a part of all the men she ever slept with inside of her. That is why some men don't know whether they were

"The First Steps"

coming or going because they're missing those parts of themselves of what they deposit into the woman they slept with. The woman couldn't get it together because they were walking around with all the men they slept with.

The woman slept with a man who was a homosexual she would have that sprit in her. She would begin to wonder why she is looking at woman and know that's not her thing. Well I knew God had done a cleansing in me from sex, smoking and drinking

Done with my shacking relationship I'm now left in a situation where I have to believe God for His every word. I always believed if I had a good man I would be ok. My family was doing their own thing and I was pretty much on my own. My girlfriend offered me to stay with her but I was go grateful for her dragging me to church I didn't want to mess up our relationship. She lived with someone anyway and she worked the overnight shift. Her working schedule meant I would be home alone with her man. I didn't want any parts in that and besides she had a cat and I am petrified of cats!

One of my old girlfriends from around the way had come with me to the baptism and got baptized too. So I wound up staying with her for a few days. She was trying to walk with God too but it just wasn't happening as fast for her as it did with me. She still had some struggles and me being so young in the Lord I had to be focus and didn't need any temptations around. So eventually my big cousin who was always at my rescue let me stay with her. She had been walking with God now for a while and was over joyed that He had found me. She was so amazed at what and how fast God was moving in my life.

She was encouraging me to stay with God because she is one of the people who know me and where I come from. So I continued my involvement in church just about every night we had something to do. A few weeks later we went on a women's retreat in upstate New York. My friend from around the way came and we hooked up with these two girls that had been going to church. They were young and from the hood like us and we had an awesome time in the Lord!

It was good to relate to someone who came from the same place as we did. It was amazing to see that God can really turn your life around. We prayed and talked about the word, hiked, ate, and had fun too. Now that I knew that I could have fun in God I was really ecstatic about serving God! It was like heaven up in those mountains relaxing, seeking God and eating good meals. At night those powerful, anointed services were amazing. Words can't even describe, you just had to experience it!

I was off for the summer and just got back from this life changing retreat. I stayed focused on getting more God and filling up with Him. I didn't watch TV shows. I would watch preacher after preacher on the Christen channels. I would read my bible even thou I didn't understand what I was reading. But the pastor told us as soon as you get up in the morning pee and then pray! So that's what I did! My prayers were real short back then because I didn't quite know what to say. But I would have these long talks with God not knowing that's what prayer was! Then I would read my bible.

They told me at the church to start in the Gospels and learn of Jesus. I didn't understand too much until someone told me to pray and ask God for understanding of His word. I begin to ask God this before I read and He began to open my eyes. Whenever the bible was being taught I would take notes and go back and review my notes every night and reread the scriptures they taught from. I was getting a lot out of this because we had Sunday service at our church and at night we went to the big church.

Monday nights we had prayer non-stop. This other pastor would teach on prayer. He was a good teacher. He would give us so much and our spirits would be so full. Some of us would fall asleep sometime. We would go sometimes until 12 midnight. Tuesdays we had bible study. After a few weeks I began to go with them to the big church. We went on Wednesday nights and Sunday nights. I just wanted to stay busy with God. I didn't want to give the devil no time to lure me away.

The big church was a little different you had different nationalities and their songs were different to what I heard at my church. It was all-good and the pastor was so funny but he taught the bible so well! I loved it! On Sunday night he had different preachers come and it was so good for me to be exposed to different preachers. Thursdays we had the woman support night.

The Day I Died but Now Live!

Most Fridays we would go to one of the sister's house and get our hair done and Saturday we had to set up for Sunday! Some nights we finished late and the pastor would let me stay the night instead of traveling back to Paterson so late by myself. She wasn't having a good feeling about me being in Paterson at this stage in my life. I knew what she meant. I wasn't trying to go around or see the people I hung out with. But if I did I would preach to them especially my family.

My nephew was getting all caught up in that gang life and one night I jumped out the car that was blasting Mary Mary gospel songs and told him he must give his heart to Jesus. I wanted him to be saved from this mess! He laughed and thought it was funny. So I kept it moving. The day I got baptized I rode pass the barbershop I hung out at every day. I stopped to see this guy who was like my best friend; he worked there and hadn't seen me all week.

I said I owed him that much to explain where I been and where I'm going from now on. It was also an opportunity to share the good news of Jesus Christ. Again I jumped out the car hype and said I just wanted to let yall know I'm saved now. God saved me and took away the desire to smoke from me.

"It's been four days and I haven't smoked!" I confessed. That was a big accomplishment because I was high every day!

My boys were high. They said, "Four days Re no smoking! Wow! That's good keep it up and we wish you the best! But we aint trying to hear that!"

But a seed was sown and God was doing the rest. After a few more weeks one of my other friends whom I was really close with called and said "what's up? I called the New York number and he said you bounced!" I told her I was in the dentist and I would come to the projects to speak to her. We were very close and I didn't want her to worry. So cautiously I went to the projects to fill her in.

As soon as I pulled up a guy who was like a cousin and brother to me started yelling "Yo B—Where you been B—!"

"Oh My God!" I exclaimed. I wasn't used to that anymore! But funny that was one of my favorite words and I called everybody. But it wasn't me anymore God had also cleaned me from that nasty mouth of mines.

So my friend got in the car with me and she said "What's up what going on? Where you been? Where are you living?" I began to explain what was happening to me and all God had done. She received it well and was very happy for me telling me to keep praying for her and that she had news too! She informed me of her new affiliation!

I said, "Wow another thing God has saved me from because if he didn't I would probably be right with her."

As far as my living situation by this time after so many times staying the night I had moved in with the pastor.

Chapter Twelve

"Church Life"

". . . . Entreat me not to leave thee, or to return from following after thee: for whither thou lodges, I will lodge: thou people shall be my people, and thy God my God" (Ruth 1:16 KJV)

I was now living with the pastor and neither she nor I knew why. She hadn't planned on anyone living with her again and I didn't plan on living with anybody else. We just understood that this was the plan of God! She had a faithful group of girls who took care of her or helped her out with whatever she needed. I didn't know anything about church culture because I was a street minded female but when I needed to be educated I let it out.

One of the girls knew me from her brothers but we didn't know each other like that. But we had a lot in common. She was the type of person who would make people feel comfortable and kept it real. She would help anybody with anything. She was with the pastor the most. One of them stayed with the Pastor in church and served her in church and served her well with excellence another one who was like the glue between them. She had come from a church background and schooled them on a lot of things. It was a few more but those were the main three. The other girls didn't understand who I was and how did I get so close to live with the pastor. When I started to stay the night some nights the pastor had already told me to stay and the other girls would tell me to go home. I would cry all the way back to Paterson wondering why these church girls treated me like this. Am I doing something wrong?

I had a lot to learn but I was trying my best to be all of what God wanted me to be! I went to visit my sister in jail and told her I gave my life to Christ and often prayed for her. Just like my mother she had always been a spiritual person. She had some type of relationship with God in spite of all her mess. She promised when she came out she would come to church with me. I brought her a few times. She would sit there and nod out the whole time. I tried not to be embarrassed and just appreciate she was there and believe That God was doing something!

So we stayed in contact and one day she called to tell me she was in the hospital. I asked what she needed and she wanted to hear that Mary Mary song "I just want to Praise Him". I had one dollar to my name but I was going to get it for her. That night we had prayer and I asked for special prayer for my sister. That same night I woke up out of a dream that disturbed me. I jumped up crying and called the Pastor and told her I saw my sister in a casket!

"Does this mean she is going to die?" I asked.

"No Serenia", she answered.

She began to bind that death sprit. When I laid back down God began to show me all that my sister done for me in helping raising me. I felt so appreciative even though we had our ups and downs. I was going to that hospital to tell her that I recognized all she's done and thank her. Tell her how much I appreciated her and the good job she's done.

Someone gave me the tape with the song on it. I went to a store in Paterson and attempted to use a credit card that I knew didn't have available credit on it to buy her a Walkman (cassette player) and it worked! I took it as a door opening from God. I had packed some goodies Pastor had on her table and took that dollar and brought a dollar worth of candy. I was prayed up and ready to go especially to thank my sister and share the word of God.

When I got there she was so happy! I gave her the bag and she passed the goodies and went straight for the song. She put those earphones on and began to sing! "Take the shackles off my feet so I could dance". The nurse had to come close the door because she was so loud giving God praise. We talked. I expressed my gratitude and opened my bible to share.

I had an even better spiritual conversation that was talking about the armor Of God! She began to quote King James Version to me and sang some old hymns. She stared telling me how she has given her life to God and he delivered her. She said someone came up to the hospital with drugs and she refused it. She showed a difference inside.

I told her we were praying for last night and God answered our prayers and heard her cry. It was so awesome! I told her I was going up to the mountain with my Pastor and the camp. I even promised that I would see her when I got back. I had been helping my Pastor with the kids at the big church camp. It was time to end the summer off by going to the mountain with the campers. We had a good time up there for the entire summer. I started and ended my summer up in that mountain.

When we returned from the trip reality set in for me it was back to work and commuting from Newark. I had my cell phone cut off and was so busy I couldn't call my sister. I assumed everything was good because she didn't call me either. After three weeks, Pastor and another sister started asking for my sister. I had to call her. It was September 25, 2000.

Her number was in my old cell phone. After school I went over to call her right away. The guy she was staying with told us they were trying to reach me. They said softly, "Sorry to tell you Theresa has passed away. September 5th."

Immediately I didn't believe it. I said, "What, Where is her body and what happened?"

He said they found her dead and they took her body somewhere. I called my cousin and she said she would call me back. She never called

The Day I Died but Now Live!

back she just came home to tell me it was true. I was in shock and wanted to go back to my Pastor's house.

On the way there I thanked God for allowing me to be here to say goodbye. We had such an awesome time not knowing it would be my last. I had peace because I knew she was with God because I knew before she left this earth she got it right with God! But I would miss her and knew her son would take it hard! When I reached to my Pastor's house I broke down I crawled up into her arms like a little baby and she prayed for me. I cried so much it eventually calmed me down.

I was so out of it they forced me to drink water and chew bread. The next day one of the faithful girls came with Pastor and I to identify her body. I was so scared to do something like this but I knew I had to do what I had to do. My cousin helped me make the funeral arrangements. The funeral director was able to take care of everything through welfare.

That night at bible study, my friends from work came giving me money for flowers and clothes. I was so grateful. It was my birthday and now every birthday I was going to remember mourning my sister. Well God woke me up with such joy and grace to go and shop for her clothing. My Pastor and the Pastor who taught us on prayer did the funeral. She looked really pretty and everything turned out good. My nephew was locked up. I had to let them tell him. This was so hard for me because I wanted to be there for him. But they moved to a more secure jail because they were afraid he would try to get out. They let him come view her body before we got there. I was so sorry he had to be by himself.

When everything was over The Bishop of our church told me, "God is a God of life the enemy has stolen your sister so get even with the devil!" meaning serve God with you whole heart and win many souls for the kingdom. This is what I did!

Chapter Thirteen

"Fire"

"And when all the children of Isreal saw how the fire came down, and the glory of the Lord upon the house, they bowed themselves with their faces to the ground upon the pavement, and worshiped, and praised the Lord, saying For He is good: for His mercy endureth forever" (2Chronicles 7:3KLV)

I was seeking God wholeheartedly. I still wanted to know more about God. Since I was off for the summer I had time to spend seeking God hard through prayer, fasting and of course the Word of God. I stayed in church and when I wasn't I was reading, praying, watching Christian TV or doing something with my Pastor. Being with her was like being in church; she was always visiting the sick, praying for people who called and counseling them. If anyone came around I don't care if they were the garbage man she would ask them if they knew Jesus and if they didn't 99% of the time they would know Him after she got done talking to them. After a summer of living like this I was so on fire for the Lord! I was so zealous that I couldn't understand how some older Christians couldn't believe God more! I was such a baby in Christ. Everything I asked for I got. Until one day I went to the Mercedes Benz dealer and laid hands on a truck I couldn't afford! Ahhhhh that was a wake-up call for me that God was not a hocus pocus God! Whatever I prayed for that was his will he gave me!

I wanted so bad to be filled with the Holy Ghost with evidence of speaking in tongues. One Monday I fasted and prayed all day with high hopes that at prayer that night I would be filled up with speaking tongues. Well I did and you really couldn't tell me anything now! I was officially filled with the Holy Ghost! As I rolled with my Pastor, I began to do what she did: pray for people, witness to people and share my testimony. I think one reason God allowed me to live with her so that I could really see He was real. She practiced what she preached. The entire time I lived with her I never seen her get out of character. Her phone rang all times a night and she would answer it, "Praise the Lord!" It didn't matter if it was a convict calling collect or a long time member of the church. She would take the time out for them.

As God began to heal me He used my Pastor to be a motherly guide for me. This was probably another reason I had to stay with her for a while. The little things like rolling her hair up at night and being able to go in her pocket book made me feel like a daughter. Her family even began to include me in their family.

When I went back to work my coworkers were still amazed. Two weeks before I got saved I went to happy hour with them and got drunk as a skunk and here I was two weeks later waving saying" Praise the Lord!" They thought I had lost it! After a whole summer passed I was still praising the Lord. It was for real this time but they didn't know how to take me. Anytime I had an ear or an opportunity I would witness to people. I even lead a Jehovah witness to Jesus.

I worked so hard that year at my job with a brand new teacher. I taught her a lot of things and it was noticed by everybody even my principal encouraged me to go get my teaching license. I had already started the process. I had taken the test twice and missed it by one point. I was scheduled to take it again but this time I had Jesus. After taking it the third time a Jewish teacher asked, "How was the test?"

I said "I passed". She said how do you know already? It takes eight weeks to get the results back. My response was the Bible says to speak those things that are not as thou they were!" So I passed in Jesus name.

She was speechless. I did pass and my principle was ready to give me a teaching job and interviewed me. Once Human Resources reviewed my paperwork they informed the principal that my college GPA wasn't high enough. The director was inexperienced and didn't know how to handle

"Fire"

this situation. My principal called me in very cautiously to tell me that Human Resources said they couldn't hire me.

She knew from previous experiences with me that I was the type to blow up. We had a meeting at our school; one time with board member and I cursed one of them out because the lady called me ignorant. She also attempted to withhold my increment (my yearly raise). I wrote a letter that was very detailed I couldn't even believe I wrote it and cc'd it to the Assistant Superintendent. The news about me not being hired had leaked.

I praised God! If God closed the door He is going to open a bigger and better one! She was so shocked that I didn't blow up. It ministered to her and this time she seen how God changed me. I continued to work faithfully the rest of that year and confessed that this would be my last year. Well that summer I bumped into a friend from college who just got hired in the Irvington school district. I told him my situation and he said you should check Irvington out maybe they can hire you. I went to speak to Human Resources and they informed me that that GPA requirement didn't apply to the preschool to third grade teacher's certification. I decided to apply with the state to get my certificate of eligibility which would enable me to apply for teaching jobs. Once I had that and if something came available he would call me.

Well you know it was a process for all the paperwork to get back so I had to go back to work in September. People couldn't wait to say, "I thought you weren't coming back?"

My response was, "I'll be leaving soon just waiting on some paper work."

I kept hearing in my spirit October 5th. I didn't know what was going to happen that day. God answered. On October 5th my certificate came and a job was available.

I had to give Paterson a 45 day resignation notice. It wasn't kindergarten but it was a foot in the door. I had a job at a school that I rode pass every morning teaching fourth grade. I'll never forget those last few months especially that September 11th. That was about the only time I had lost my cool. Our country was being attacked and I need to get back to Newark with the saints!

God didn't leave me hanging. I was happy to inform my curious coworkers too. I got a teaching job and I would be making six thousand more than I would have made working in Paterson. Shortly after that God said it was time for my Pastor to release this little bird out the nest to fly on her own. I knew it was time to go even though so many times I thought she would literally throw me out. I had been thrown out so many times before. I was expecting her to do the same.

She told tell me so many times, "Serenia I'm not those people who will throw you out." She didn't make moves unless God told her too.

Chapter Fourteen

"New Season"

"To everything there is a season, and a time to every purpose under the heavens: Ecclesiastes **(3:1KJV)**

NOW was the time for me to really walk in those things I had learned. I was teaching fourth grade in another school district. New people meant rules. It was a different culture at this school. At my old school we were so close. My old coworkers even gave me a big moving on party. It was so nice. I loved the fact that we were all different nationalities and come from different professional backgrounds. We ate lunch together, knew each other birthdays and children too!

At this new school I noticed right away that it was very racially separated. Black people stayed with the black people and white people stayed with the white people. I was nice to everyone but wasn't use to the separation. Then a weird thing happened. I formed a relationship with the teacher whose class I took over. One day she and few other women approached me questioning my credentials. I was a little intimidated at first but really got pissed that they questioned my integrity. I went home and prayed. I prayed for them too.

It was the beginning of the year and I was teaching third grade. The next day after praying for these women I was offered to switch with a teacher to teach first grade. My plan was set to teach kindergarten but it was so close that I was overjoyed. There was a misunderstanding that the district would pay for classes to complete my teacher's certification. So I had already registered for my alternate route classes at Kean College.

Unfortunately, I didn't find out until after the add-drop period that the district wasn't going to pay so I ended up dropping the courses and owed Kean College five hundred dollars. Because of this delay, I just couldn't afford five hundred dollars on top of tuition. My budget was tight. At the same time I started a new position, moved into my own apartment along with a lot of debt I created before I came to the Lord. The delay in not taking classes finally caught up with me. Human Resources contacted me and told me I had to be in classes by September or they would let me go.

As I was starting to learn, God showed up when again. One of my coworkers I had grew close to offered to pay the five hundred dollars so I could register for class. I was elated. When I went to register for class I found out about a program that would pay for my classes only if I took them on the weekend! There I was in class all day on Saturday but it was a great program.

So now I had a lot going from my professional career to living on my own as a single woman. I continued living a full life of ministry. I was barely home because of class but when I was home I enjoyed the time I had alone with the Lord! I had a somewhat empty room and I would play music and dance before the Lord. I would have some good pray time. When the girls came over we would watch Juanita Bynum tapes and have church. A lot of things that we decreed came to pass. The meetings took place at my apartment with planning events or have fellowships. I would have the single meetings at my apartment to plan events or have fellowships. Sometimes I would have sleep over's with little girls or teenagers. I loved for people to come over so I could cook.

I had my moments living here too. I gave myself a year to pay off some old debt but I got behind on my car payments. One morning I went outside to go to work and the car was gone. I was shocked and a little disappointed. But I shook the dust off my feet, went back inside and put some sneakers on praised God and walked the short distance to work.

Walking was my new transportation to work until one of the teacher's brothers gave me his hoopty. I was so grateful someone gave me a car. It worked for a little while then died. My Pastor granddaughter got a new car so she gave me her current car. I was just grateful again I had another car given to me. That car worked for a while too then it started acting crazy.

The Day I Died but Now Live!

I had to put my hand out to do signals that I wasn't even sure I was doing it right. It was honking and smoking and all types of stuff until one day I said enough! This is not God for me to drive around like this!

During lunch time at work I decided that I was going to get a car. I had no money, bad credit you name it. I believed God was going to help me. I shared with one of my prayer partners and friend at work and she came with me. I went to the Toyota dealer and went for the top of the line! The sales person told me I wasn't approved. We walked around the lot again and that quick I remembered having a vision driving a red car. I stood right in front of a red Camary.

"This is it. I'm taking this one home", I told the salesman excitedly. My faith was high and totally dependent on God to purchase this car off the lot. I stumbled back and forth thinking about the money.

She busted out and said, "I can loan you five hundred dollars". Well I was put on the spot. So, now I had to give five hundred dollars too. So with a thousand dollar down payment I was able to leave with my car. I knew again God was working. Today I still have my red Camary but her time is limited. I'm going to sale it soon and believe God will show me another vision for a car.

Sometimes I had little lonely moments. I would come home at night in my dark and quiet apartment. It was definitely good times to think and praise God. Honestly, I would have thoughts wondering how my apartment would be if I had a man with some little baby feet running around in it.

I lived a holy single life! I was married to the Lord in every way. I didn't have any time for conversation with any jokers! I had decided I was saving the cookies for my husband. I knew God would bless me one day with the right person. I remembered the bible said, "He that finds a wife finds a good thing." He would find me and I would be good.

Being a good thing was my focus. People thought I was crazy for not talking on the phone or going places to meet people. Honestly knowing my past, I was totally scared of the idea of picking someone. I wanted a man that God had for me. Oh, the devil did try to get back in my life challenging me on this.

A young man that came to the church occasionally had helped me before with some repairs on the hoopty cars. We had to exchanged numbers and little by little those car conversations left talking about cars to praying for him and I thought he was for me. He had just had a baby and already had about five kids while on probation. I told my Pastor and she said, "Oh no cut it off now!"

Well I was upset at first thinking she didn't want me to be with anyone. I talked to another Pastor she trusted to teach us and he had the same response. So I cut it off and came to my senses that I was bugging.

My Pastor other grand daughter and her family lived next door to me. She was the one who told us about the apartment. This was another testimony. When I went to look at the apartment I didn't have much of security saved up. But the land lord gave me a good price and let me pay the security deposit in payments and I was able to get the keys and move in right away. I had no furniture but by the end of month I had all I needed. Nothing like being a child of God! Soon after my Pastor's granddaughter and her husband began to believe God for a house. After I heard that I heard God say buy a house warming card and sow five hundred dollars. This wasn't something I couldn't afford to do but as always I had to obey God. Eventually they brought a house in a neighboring town which was right around the corner. So now I was totally on my own in this apartment. My upstairs neighbor was my landlord's nephew who was a single professional too. He was a nice guy and would look out for me. I just had to remind him that not only do you have single woman down here. But one that is trying to be kept so don't get so loud up there with your girl! He was a little embarrassed but he received it and helped me out and I never heard anything else. This apartment was a stepping stone to build my faith to the level God was trying to get me to.

Chapter Fifteen

"Family"

"Wherefore I desire that ye faint not at my tribulations for you, which is your glory. For this cause I bow my knees unto the father of our Lord Jesus Christ, Of whom the whole family in heaven and earth is named. (Ephesians3:13-15KJV)

Living alone single wasn't the only thing that kept me humble. After I was going through the loss of my sister I had to focus on her son. He was young and back and forth from being incarcerated. I also had my big brother who I hadn't seen or been in contact with since I been saved and losing our sister. This was the second time I would have to break news to him about something that happened months ago. I didn't know how to contact him when our mom died and now I wasn't able to contact him about our sister. I began to pray that God would connect us again somehow! I also prayed for my sister's son that he would surrender and give his heart to God. He was always in and out of jail more so when he was getting more and more involved in the street life and drugs. The same path I saw my sister take.

I began to immediately pray against everything going on. Fred Hammond sang a song "Late in the midnight hour God is going to turn it around!" I use to sing this song with such passion knowing God was going to do it for my family. So one night he did it! I got a phone call from my nephew in the middle of the night to come and get him now from Paterson. I was so sleepy.

My Pastor declared, "You better go get that boy and bring him here and we will figure out something."

On the way to Paterson all I could hear was that song "LATE IN THE MIDNIGHT HOUR GOD IS GONNA TURN IT AROUND." That's exactly what he was doing. As soon as I got off the exit he was right there waiting for me! He had been beaten up badly and basically saying he surrenders! I brought him to Newark we found somewhere for him to stay for now.

Shortly after that my brother found me. He also came to Newark and we found somewhere for him to stay. They were there with me in church even though they couldn't sit still the whole service putting their hands to the plow. God started opening doors for them. My nephew had some warrants but we convinced him to go turn himself in. We took him to a couple of different counties and no one could find any warrants! They both looked for jobs and tried some schooling. My Pastor helped them get an apartment around the corner from her. I was so happy we were all together. Neither one of them had ever had their own apartment before. They were struggling to get along.

After I moved into my apartment they would come visit me. I knew I couldn't handle either one of them living with me because even though they was going to church they didn't take it as serious as I did. I didn't listen to worldly music anymore. One time I came home and my nephew was playing Jay Z. Even thou I was a big fan before I did not want this music playing in my house. Another time I came home and found ashes on my front window seal. I knew it was tobacco they fell out of a blunt (a weed cigar). Oh he denied it over and over again. Until years later he admits that it wasn't weed but angel dust. Whatever it was he still had to go.

Small things continued to happen. I logged onto my computer and there was pornography all over the screen. I almost had a heart attack! Oh how we need grace to deal with our family members. My nephew was in and out of the church and his former girlfriend became his wife. They decided they wanted to get it right and didn't want to shack up anymore. I respected that and God put it on my heart to pay for their wedding. It was beautiful. They stayed around for a while and then moved to Pennsylvania. They endured a lot of challenges during their marriage; they moved back to New Jersey and ended up separating. Today he is still dealing with a lot of issues. I still believe God will restore him and that he would totally surrender his life to God! It shall be in JESUS name!

My brother still was in and out church and then finally went back to New York. One time a group of us went to a gospel concert at Madison Square Garden. While walking through Penn station my own brother walked right passed me. I was so hurt. I don't know if he was embarrassed or too high to see me. He would call time to time. I never really knew all what was going on with him. I think he was living on the streets and between shelters and prison. When he would make his way in to the system he would definitely contact me with a list of things he wanted. When he was in jail he would be so on fire for the Lord. The last time he was in jail after a few months he had gotten really sick.

The doctors called and told me he had stage four colon cancer. Immediately, I prayed. I had to believe God. We began to keep him in prayer. I visited him in the hospital a couple of times. The doctors tried chemotherapy but it wasn't working for him. It was a little stressful because it was so hard for me to find anything out. Sometimes weeks would pass by and I wouldn't know how he was doing. Then I finally talked to the head nurse. She explained that he was in hospice and getting pretty weak.

When I was able to get her on the phone she would let me know what was going on. I was on winter break and planned to visit him after Christmas. Well, the day after Christmas I hurt my back and could hardly walk. I was in the bed for a few days. That same day I started to feel better.

"Family"

I got a call. It was a Rabbi from the prison to let me know my brother had passed away. Every time someone from that jail would call me I was hoping to hear about a positive turn around.

But God is still good. I know my brother knew the Lord and I would see him again. I don't know if it's because he was my last immediate family I had to bury but I had a hard time. I had a memorial service at my church for him. A few days later I went to the prison to bury him up there. It only been a few months but I was dreading and still dealing with the painful heartache. God used me to lead them to Him and the rest was up to Him. God has a purpose and plan for everything!

Chapter Sixteen

"Walking By Faith"

For we walk by faith, and not by sight 2 Corinthians 5:7 KJV

After living in my apartment a few years and "God giving me strategy to get out of debt and fix my credit, it was time for me to step out on faith and go for that house! Every time I drove through affluent neighborhoods with nice houses I would wonder who lived in those houses and what kind of jobs they had. Why can't I have one my father owns the cattle on a thousand hills. So I started working on a pre-approval for a mortgage. Then my Pastor granddaughter who used to live next door had a new baby and needed to get a bigger house. So while she started looking for a new home she asked if I was interested in buying her home. It was nearby and just right for a single woman. I went and checked it out and decided to go for it. I had a peace in my spirit.

She was such a blessing and helped every step of the way. She literally held my hand through the whole process! I told her she should do this for a living! She was younger than me and was helping me. While we were waiting for our closing I had to move out my apartment and stay with my Pastor again for a month until closing. She closed shortly after me.

I was able to reap from that five hundred dollar seed I had sown to her and her family. Not only did she help me sooo much but they offered to pay closing cost which was five thousand and even threw in some furniture.

Now I had a car payment and a mortgage, I was in awe of what God had done. I had a house warming and was able to hook up my new home and make it my own. I was so grateful because God had done it again! I had to get adjusted to being a home owner and loved doing these home projects when I could.

After a year I was beginning to get a little antsy about being single! My faith was running a little low and I started to entertain the devil by listening to his lies! Thinking I was foolish for not getting out to meet someone and that I was in church too much and always with my Pastor! A guy I worked with use to say little things to me. I would never feed into it and remind him that I was waiting on my husband and no one else. He was a bold person and knew what I was about but he still would shoot his little comments in there.

The Day I Died but Now Live!

He didn't believe in Jesus and wasn't trying to hear it! We got in so many debates about religion and Jesus. Until I realized that I wasn't supposed to debate and I was throwing my pearls to the swine. When I started getting antsy every now and then I would call him or acted like I need help with something at my house. He knew a lot of people and always had someone who could help me out. Eventually I gave in to going out to dinner with him.

We drove to the shore to check on his boat and stopped to eat and came right back! I was so uncomfortable the whole time because I knew I was treading dangerous water. I had cooked for him a couple of times and it was so awkward because we had absolutely nothing in common. He was somebody that I would have dealt with in the past but way out of my league now. I was so close to falling into a situation with him. But thank God for his grace and Mercy. HE KEPT ME!

Now I know why I was so antsy the devil was trying to make me miss my blessing! I was able to get through that spring and summer. That fall was the appointed time to be found by my Boaz! Early in October I was at the big church anniversary. At the end of the service everyone went up to hug our Bishop for fathering us!

My Pastor was the only woman Pastor at the time and some of the other Pastors were like fathers to me too. So I went and hugged them too. The Pastor whose church was in Paterson was my last stop and when I hugged him he stared to say something to me and he stopped and said I have to talk to your Pastor! I always was grateful for him because of the great work he was doing in Paterson my hometown! He always supported me in different things I was involved in!

Once he came and taught the singles and his wife made me a cake and I cried! I felt so special. Well He did speak to my Pastor and told her he believe that I'm his brother's wife! My Pastor doesn't go with nothing unless she hears from God herself! She prayed and had a peace! In the mean time I knew nothing about what was going on! Until one day on my way out I asked her if she ever talk to the Pastor from Paterson and what was going on?

From the look on her face and the smile she gave me I knew it was something big and special! So I continued to pick and pick until she told me! I took it in and kept moving. We went to the anniversary. Shortly after the anniversary ended his brother walked us to the car with an umbrella. After He said "can I speak to you for a moment." In my mind I was saying what is this joker doing? I don't mess around like this! But I said "ok"! I went to the side and spoke to him. He said "I have been praying and fasting and God showed me that you are my wife!" Well I could have hit the floor. I didn't know what to say but "ok if God told you that then He will speak to me too!" So I was praying and fasting like crazy. A few weeks later he talked to my Pastor on the phone and she gave her blessing and my number! He called me and I was in Atlantic City at a teacher conference and we talked until my battery died. I wanted to know more about him.

We went out to Star-bucks and talked for hours. I felt so comfortable and I was able to be myself.

Now I was really listening for God! We continued to talk and take in a movie now and then. One day I was by a friend of mine house cooking and listening to music. The Holy Ghost fell on me and I heard God say "what have you been asking for?" "Why are you afraid? Go forth my daughter!" I flew out that door to go tell my Pastor that I heard God ok this! We continued to get to know each other but knowing we both heard God we statred making plans.

We were very careful in our dating! He would never step foot in my house. Not even to use the bathroom. We did a lot of praying. We both had waited on God for so long and didn't want to mess anything up! The night he planned to officially propose with a ring. I decided I wanted to go the movies. But all along he knew what his plan was and he tried to convince me it wasn't a good night to go. I though he just didn't want to go. His son was interested in going so we went together. Well it was still a glorious night! When I brought his son home he came out and got in car and we talked awhile and then he popped the question! I was so shocked! Even thou I knew it was about to go down. I couldn't believe it. It was official I was on my way to becoming Mrs. Farrell.

Both of our Pastors counseled us and in six months we were married. We had a beautiful park wedding and nice reception! We didn't really have the money to pull this off but what God starts, He will finish. People began to sow like crazy. Someone brought my dress, someone made my hair piece, even down to chairs for the park everything was paid for! The only thing that was difficult was making the guest list! We both come from big churches and were in leadership. But we got through it! The photographer even blessed us! It was in May so the weather was a little shaky. My dream was to have an outside wedding and as long as Wayne and our Pastors were there it was going to be a wedding. It was a little cloudy and on my way to get my make-up done it started pouring down raining.

Wayne called me and asked "What do I want him to do" I said "tell them to wipe off the chairs and I'm on my way". As soon as I arrived at the park the sun came out. The grass was a little damp and people had their umbrellas out. But my tall dark Trinidadian was waiting at the bottom of the hill with our Pastors. My nephew and I got out the car and walked down the aisle which was down a hill to the groom and crowd. The big event was over and now time for honeymoon!

We had a nice honeymoon in Florida. A few months later we decided to try for a baby and around October I was pregnant with our first baby girl Nyla and two years later came baby girl number two Milan. God is so good I was blessed with this great man of God and a teenage son and my two baby girls. A family that God put together! God has restored all that was stolen from me! To God Be all The Glory For what He has done!

About the Author

Serenia Farrell born was Serenia Redmond at St. Joseph Hospital in Paterson, NJ to Dolores Redmond in 1972. Being born in an unexpected, premature and breeched pregnancy is when Serenia began her life's journey of bringing God glory. Surrounded by despair and unfortunate circumstances she was able to escape what statistics might have predicted as a hopeless future. Not knowing God had predestined her to greatness despite her obstacles. In June 2000 Serenia began her relationship with Jesus Christ and her eyes were opened to her real destiny and purpose of life. She was able to see that it was God that brought her though all of life's difficulties and set her before greatness despite of what was predicted. Her insurmountable hurdles lead her to believe she was a mistake, worthless and insignificant. But God mapped a plan that intercepted that and was able to accomplish great things throughout her. Serenia has been able to be the first to graduate high school in her family, earning her college degree with no stable residency, establishing a professional career in elementary education, mentor, and most of all a true servant of God.

Serenia earned her Bachelor's of Art in Communication concentrating in Television Production and a minor in African American Studies at Ramapo Collage. Currently she teaches first grade for Irvington Public Schools. June 2000 to May 2007 she had devoted her life to serving in various ministries such as singles, prison, evangelizing team and closely serving where needed at Love of Jesus Family Church of Newark, NJ. Currently she worships at Love of Jesus World Outreach Center in Paterson, NJ as a devoted wife and mother of three lovely children.